MEMOIRS

The Ludwig von Mises Institute dedicates
this volume to all of its generous donors
and wishes to thank these Patrons, in particular:

Mary and Bill Braum
Hugh E. Ledbetter

❖❖❖

Todd Gibson
Frederick L. Maier

❖❖❖

Mr. and Mrs. Wesley B. Alexander, Ross K. Anderson, Anonymous, David Atherton, Mr. and Mrs. David Baumgardner, Steven R. Berger, John Hamilton Bolstad, Mr. and Mrs. J. Robert Bost, Wayne Chapeskie, Dan H. Courtney, Mr. and Mrs. Jeremy S. Davis, Kevin P. Duffy, Evans Cabinet Corp., Mr. and Mrs. Brian Gladish, Paul F. Glenn, Keith M. Harnish, Bernard G. Koether II, Hunter Lewis, Arthur L. Loeb, Mr. and Mrs. William Lowndes III, Mr. and Mrs. William W. Massey, Jr., Joseph Edward Paul Melville, Robert A. Moore, Terence Murphree, Mr. and Mrs. R. Nelson Nash, Laurence A. Peterson, Mr. and Mrs. Ronald L. Peterson, Mr. William D. Plumley, Mr. and Mrs. Wilfried A. Puscher, Ann V. Rogers, Sheldon Rose, Thomas S. Ross, Norman K. Singleton, Mr. and Mrs. Dennis A. Sperduto, Donnie R. Stacy, M.D., James R. Von Ehr, Dr. Thomas L. Wenck, James M. Wolfe

MEMOIRS

LUDWIG VON MISES

TRANSLATED BY ARLENE OOST-ZINNER

LvMI

Ludwig von Mises Institute

For information write the Ludwig von Mises Institute, 518 West Magnolia Avenue, Auburn, Alabama 36832. Mises.org.

ISBN: 978-1-933550-26-8

Contents

Preface

Ludwig von Mises is the author of dozens of books and hundreds of articles in which he made pioneering contributions to economics, history, the philosophy of science, and social philosophy. He had a direct personal influence on many outstanding social scientists such as F.A. Hayek, Fritz Machlup, Oskar Morgenstern, Gottfried von Haberler, Hans Sennholz, Murray Rothbard, George Reisman, Ralph Raico, Leonard Liggio, Israel Kirzner, Paul Cantor, and others who attended his seminars from the 1920s to the 1960s. In the interwar period he was also a major economic advisor to the government in his native Austria.

And yet, today we still know amazingly few things about this man. Much if not most of what we know is based on the present autobiographical recollections, which Mises started to write upon his arrival in the United States in August 1940. By the end of that year he had finished a first draft of the German-language manuscript and then polished his memoirs for another two years. Finally he gave the handwritten text to his wife Margit for custody and eventual publication. In 1978, five years after his death, she published both the German original and an English translation from the pen of Hans Sennholz.[1]

---

[1]See Mises, *Erinnerungen von Ludwig v. Mises* (Stuttgart: Gustav Fischer, 1978); idem *Notes and Recollections* (South Holland, Ill.: Libertarian

The memoirs cover his intellectual development from youth to 1940. Thus they are essential and fascinating reading for all students of Austrian economics and of the history of ideas.

They are similarly important for students of world politics in the twentieth century. In fact, Mises's memoirs are a unique source of inside information about the economics and politics of the first Republic of Austria. They portray his professional life from about 1906 (year when he graduated with a doctorate in law from the University of Vienna) to 1940, stressing his activities in the Vienna Chamber of Commerce, in World War I, in government, and in academia. He not only knew the intellectuals of his day, he had almost daily interaction with the political leaders of his country, with the higher echelons of the civil service, and with the executives of Austrian firms and business corporations. Today this might seem to be largely irrelevant local history, but in fact it is not. The little Republic of Austria was the heiress of the great Habsburg Empire that had just crumbled in 1918. In the 1920s and 1930s, the country still played an important role in world politics, most notably in its opposition to the burgeoning political movements of Bolshevism and National Socialism. It is not exaggerated to say that one cannot fully grasp world politics in the twentieth century without a thorough understanding of Austrian politics in the interwar period. The present memoirs are a precious key to such understanding. They are unique in that their author was not just an insider, but an insider who understood the key economic issues of his time far better than most other protagonists.[2]

Press, 1978). Meanwhile, translations into the Italian, Spanish, and French languages have been published: *Autobiografia di un liberale* (Soveria Mannelli: Rubettino, 1996); *Autobiografía de un Liberal* (Madrid: Unión Editorial, 2001); *Souvenirs d'Europe* (http://herve.dequengo.free.fr/Mises/SE/SE.htm).

[2]Mises is today mainly known for his contributions to economic theory. But he is also an important historian of contemporary totalitarian

What do the memoirs tell us about their author? What does Mises reveal about himself? Not much. He essentially confines himself to a narration of his intellectual development and public life. There is no word on the following pages about his dreams and feelings, love affairs, personal income and wealth, passions, and temptations; no word about daily family life or his attitudes toward parents, brothers, house personnel, cousins, teachers, or neighbors; no word about car accidents or broken legs.

This is fully in line with his other writings and personal records. Even in his letters he handled such private matters with great discretion. All through his life he studiously avoided writing and publishing about himself, even though he played a rather remarkable personal role as we have already noticed.[3]

Implicitly, however, the memoirs actually do tell us a few things about Mises the man.

---

movements. See in particular Mises, *Nation, State, and Economy* (1919); idem, *Omnipotent Government* (1944); idem, *Planned Chaos* (1947). His very first publications as a young scholar (1902–1906) also dealt with historical problems, though in those days he was under the influence of historicist and interventionist ideas which he later rejected, as explained in the present work.

[3]Apart from the memoirs (which he did not publish), the only piece of writing in which Mises discussed his own ideas is an address delivered to the economics department of New York University, in November 1940, in the context of a job search in his new home country. See Mises, "My Contributions to Economic Theory," *Planning for Freedom*, 4th ed. (South Holland, Ill.: Libertarian Press, 1980), pp. 224–33. In his theoretical writings he made numerous comments on the history of ideas, but next to never on his own ideas. In the 1960s he published a small booklet on the history of the Austrian School of economics, in which he also did not get to the point of talking about himself. See Mises, *The Historical Setting of the Austrian School of Economics* (1962, 1969; reprinted Auburn, Ala.: Ludwig von Mises Institute, 1984 and 2007).

It is first of all significant that in his recollections he chose to focus exclusively on his public persona, though admittedly it is not quite clear what this focus signifies precisely. It could have been the outgrowth of anxiety or feelings of vulnerability. Mises might have feared that, in writing about his emotions, he might not be able to control language and thought as much as when writing about politics and economics. In actual fact he did not always control himself in situations of private conflict, in particular, when he had arguments with his future spouse.[4] However, the focus on his public persona could also reflect his deep-seated humility and stoic concern for disentangling matters of common interest from those of merely personal interest.

Moreover, the memoirs are unique among Mises's works in that he makes a great number of blunt statements about the persons with whom he interacted in his professional life. He had a reputation of being unable to suffer fools gladly, but he never stated these opinions in writing. As he relates in the present book, he had early on adopted the principle of never writing about the personal moral shortcomings of his opponents, and of focusing instead on their intellectual errors in order to combat the latter more effectively. Only in the memoirs—which, again, were not meant for publication during his lifetime—did he talk about virtues and vices. Now if we look at his heroes and villains, we find the reflections of a stoic value system, cherishing above all good will, hard work, and expertise, while despising avarice, pretentiousness, and shallowness.

Mises would never write an update to cover the last third of his life in America. The memoirs were a balance sheet of his

---

[4]"Occasionally he showed terrible outbursts of tantrum." Margit von Mises, *My Years with Ludwig von Mises* (New Rochelle, N.Y.: Arlington House, 1976), p. 36.

achievements in the Old World, written in the style of a testament, at the absolute low point of his life—a personal reckoning and a lesson for his future readers. May all readers of this beautiful new translation benefit from it!

Jörg Guido Hülsmann
Angers, France
February 2009

Introduction

Although without a doubt one of the most important economists of his generation, in a certain sense Ludwig von Mises remained an outsider in the academic world until the end of his unusually long scholarly career—certainly within the German-speaking world—but also during the last third of his life, when in the United States he raised a larger circle of students. Before this his strong immediate influence had essentially been restricted to his Viennese *Privatseminar*, whose members for the most part only became attracted to him once they had completed their original studies.

If it would not have unduly delayed the publication of these memoirs, found among his papers, I would have welcomed the opportunity of analyzing the reasons for this curious neglect of one of the most original thinkers of our time in the field

---

This "Introduction" by F.A. Hayek was written for the German-language edition of Mises's *Notes and Recollections* (Erinnerungen von Ludwig von Mises [Stuttgart: Gustav Fischer, 1978]). It was translated into English by Hans-Hermann Hoppe and published in the *Austrian Economics Newsletter* (Fall 1988): 1–3. It also appears in the *Fortunes of Liberalism: The Collected Works of F.A. Hayek* (Chicago: University of Chicago Press, 1992), pp. 153–59.

of economics and social philosophy. But in part the fragmentary autobiography he left provides in itself the answer. The reasons why he never acquired a chair at a German-speaking university during the twenties or before 1933, while numerous and often indisputably highly unimportant persons did, were certainly personal. His appointment would have been beneficial for every university. Yet the instinctive feeling of the professors that he would not quite fit into their circle was not entirely wrong. Even though his subject-knowledge surpassed that of most occupants of professorial chairs, he was nonetheless never a real specialist. When in the realm of the social sciences I look for similar figures in the history of thought, I do not find them among the professors, not even in Adam Smith; instead, he must be compared to thinkers like Voltaire or Montesquieu, Tocqueville and John Stuart Mill. This is an impression that has by no means been reached only in retrospect. But when more than fifty years ago I tried to explain Mises's position in pretty much the same words to Wesley Claire Mitchell in New York I only encountered—perhaps understandably—a politely ironic skepticism.

Essential to his work is a global interpretation of social development. In contrast to the few comparable contemporaries such as Max Weber, with whom he was connected by a rare mutual respect, in this Mises had the advantage of a genuine knowledge of economic theory.

The following memoirs say much more about his development, position and views than I know or could tell. I can only attempt here to supplement or confirm information regarding the ten years of his time in Vienna (1921–1931) during which I was closely associated with him. I came to him rather characteristically not as a student, but as a fresh Doctor of Law and a civil servant, subordinate to him, at one of those special institutions that had been created to execute the provisions of the peace treaty of St. Germain. The letter of recommendation by my university teacher Friedrich von Wieser, who described me as a highly promising young economist, was met by Mises with a smile and the remark that he had never seen me in his lectures.

However, when he found my interest confirmed and my knowledge satisfactory, he helped me in every regard and contributed much to make my lengthier visit to the United States possible (before the time of the Rockefeller fellowship) to which I owe a great deal. But although I saw him during the first years daily in an official capacity, I had no idea that he was preparing his great book, *Socialism,* which upon its publication in 1922 influenced me decisively.

Only after I returned from America in the summer of 1924 was I admitted to that circle, which had been in existence for some time, and through which Mises's scholarly work in Vienna mainly exerted its influence. This "Mises Seminar," as we all called the biweekly nightly discussions in his office, is described in detail in his memoirs. Mises though does not mention the hardly less important regular continuations of the official discussions that lasted long into the night at a Viennese coffeehouse. As he correctly describes, these were not instructional meetings, but discussions presided over by an older friend whose views were by no means shared by all members. Strictly speaking, only Fritz Machlup was originally Mises's student. As regards the others, of the regular members only Richard Strigl, Gottfried Haberler, Oskar Morgenstern, Lene Lieser, and Martha Stefanie Braun were specialists in economics. Ewald Schams and Leo Schönfeld, who belonged to the same highly gifted but early deceased intermediate generation as Richard Strigl, were, to my knowledge, never regular participants in the Mises Seminar. But sociologists like Alfred Schütz, philosophers like Felix Kaufmann and historians like Friedrich Engel-Janosi were equally active in the discussions, which frequently dealt with the problems of the methods of the social sciences, but rarely with special problems of economic theory (except those of the subjective theory of value). Questions of economic policy, however, were discussed often, and always from the perspective of the influence of different social philosophies upon it.

All this seemed to be the rare mental distraction of a man, who, during the day, was fully occupied with urgent political and economic problems, and who was better informed about daily polities, modern history, and general ideological developments than most others. What he was working on even I, who officially saw him almost daily during those years, did not know; he never spoke about it. We could even less imagine when he would actually write his works. I knew only from his secretary that from time to time he had a manuscript typed from his distinctively clear handwriting. But many of his works only existed in handwriting until publication, and an important article was considered lost for a long time, until it finally resurfaced among the papers of a journal editor. No one knew anything regarding his private work methods until his marriage. He did not speak about his literary activity until he had completed a work. Though he knew that I was most willing to occasionally help him, he only asked me once to look up a quote for his work and this was after I mentioned that I wanted to consult a work on the canonists in the library. He never had, at least in Vienna, a scholarly assistant.

The problems with which he concerned himself were mostly problems for which he considered the prevailing opinion false. The reader of the following book might gain the impression that he was prejudiced against the German social sciences as such. This was definitely not the case, even though in the course of time he developed a certain understandable irritation. But he valued the great early German theoreticians like Thünen, Hermann, Mangoldt or Gossen more highly than most of his colleagues, and knew them better. Also, among his contemporaries he valued a few similarly isolated figures such as Dietzel, Pohle, Adolf Weber and Passow, as well as the sociologist Leopold von Wiese and, above all, Max Weber. With Weber a close scholarly relationship had been formed during Weber's short teaching activity in Vienna, in the spring of 1918, which could have meant a great deal if Weber had not died so soon. But in general, there can be no doubt that he had nothing but contempt for the majority of the professors who, occupying the chairs of the German universities, pretended to teach theoretical economics. Mises does not exaggerate in his description of the teachings of economics as espoused by the historical school. Just how far the level of theoretical thinking in Germany had sunk is indicated by the fact that it needed the simplifications and coarseness of the—herein certainly meritorious—Swede Gustav Cassel in order to again find an audience for theory in Germany. Notwithstanding his exquisite politeness in society and his generally great self-control (he could also occasionally explode), Mises was not the man to successfully hide his contempt.

This drove him to increased isolation among professional economists generally as well as among those Viennese circles with which he had scholarly and professional contacts. He became estranged from his cohorts and fellow students when he turned away from the advancing ideas of social policy. Twenty-five years later I could still feel the emotion and anger his seemingly sudden break had caused—when he had turned away from the dominating ideals of the academic youth of the first few years of the century—when his fellow student F.X. Weiss (the editor of the shorter writings of Böhm-Bawerk) told me about the event with unconcealed indignation, obviously in order to prevent me from a similar betrayal of "social" values and an all-too-great sympathy for an "outlived" liberalism.

If Carl Menger had not aged relatively early and Böhm-Bawerk had not died so young, Mises probably would have found support among them. But the only survivor of the older Austrian School was my revered teacher Friedrich von Wieser, and he was more a Fabian—proud, as he believed, to have provided a scientific justification for progressive income taxation with his development of the theory of marginal utility.

Mises's return to classical liberalism was not only a reaction to a dominating trend. He completely lacked the adaptability of his brilliant seminar fellow Josef Schumpeter, who always quickly accommodated current intellectual fashions, as well as Schumpeter's joy in "épater le bourgeois" [shocking the middle classes]. In fact, it appeared to me as if these two most important representatives of the third generation of leading Austrian economists (one can hardly consider Schumpeter a member of the "Austrian School" in the narrower sense despite all mutual intellectual respect) both got on each other's nerves.

In today's world Mises and his students are regarded as the representatives of the Austrian School, and justifiably so, although he only represents one of the branches into which Menger's theories had already been divided by his students, and the close personal friendship between Eugen von Böhm-Bawerk and Friedrich von Wieser. I only admit this with some hesitation, because I expected much of the tradition of Wieser, which his successor Hans Mayer attempted to advance. But these expectations have not yet become fulfilled, even though those stimuli may perhaps still prove more fruitful than they have been so far. Today's active "Austrian School," almost exclusively in the United States, is at base a Mises School that goes back to Böhm-Bawerk, while the man in whom Wieser had set such great hopes and who had succeeded him in his chair never really fulfilled the promise.

Because he never occupied a regular chair in his field, in the German-speaking world, and had to devote most of his time to other-than-scholarly activities until his late fifties, Mises remained an outsider in academia. Other reasons contributed to isolating him in his position in public life and as a representative of a great social-philosophical project. A Jewish intellectual who advocated socialist ideas had his respected place in the Vienna of the first third of this century, a place that was accorded to him as a matter of course. Likewise, the Jewish banker or businessman who (bad enough!) defended capitalism had his rights. But a Jewish intellectual who justified capitalism appeared to most as some sort of monstrosity, something unnatural, which could not be categorized and with which one did not know how to deal. His undisputed subject-knowledge was impressive, and one could not avoid consulting him in critical economic situations, but rarely was his advice understood and followed. Mostly he was regarded as somewhat of an eccentric whose "old-fashioned" ideas were impracticable "today." That he himself had constructed, in long years of hard work, his own social philosophy was only known by very few and perhaps could not be understood by distant observers until 1940, when in his *Nationalökonomie* he presented for the first time his system of ideas in its entirety. But by this time he could no longer reach readers in Germany and Austria. Apart from the small circle of young theoreticians who met at his office, and some highly gifted friends in the business world who were similarly concerned about the future and who are mentioned in the following, he only encountered genuine understanding among occasional foreign visitors like the Frankfurt banker Albert Hahn, whose work in monetary theory he smiled at, however, as a vain sin of youth.

Yet he did not always make it easy for them. The arguments by which he supported his unpopular views were not always completely conclusive, even though some reflection could have shown that he was right. But when he was convinced of his conclusions and had presented them in clear and plain language—a gift that he possessed to a high degree—he believed that this would also have to convince others and only prejudice and stubbornness prevented them from understanding. For too long he had lacked the opportunity of discussing problems with intellectual equals who shared his basic moral convictions in order to see how even small differences in one's implicit assumptions can lead to different results. This manifested itself in a certain impatience that was easily suspected of being an unwillingness to understand, whereas an honest misunderstanding of his arguments was the case.

I must admit that I myself often initially did not think his arguments to be completely convincing and only slowly learned that he was mostly right and that, after some reflection, a justification could be found that he had not made explicit. And today, considering the kind of battle that he had to lead, I also understand that he was driven to certain exaggerations, like that of the *a priori* character of economic theory, where I could not follow him.

For Mises's friends of his later years, after his marriage and the success of his American activity had softened him, the sharp outbursts in the following memoirs, written at the time of his greatest bitterness and hopelessness, might come as a shock. But the Mises who speaks from the following pages is without question the Mises we knew from the Vienna of the twenties; of course without the tactful reservation that he invariably displayed in oral expression; but the honest and open expression of what he felt and thought. To a certain extent this may explain his neglect, even though it does not excuse it. We, who knew him better, were at times outraged, of course, that he did not get a chair, yet we were not really surprised. He had too much to criticize about the representatives of the profession into which he was seeking entrance to appear acceptable to them. And he fought against an intellectual wave which is now subsiding, not least because of his efforts, but which was much too powerful then for one individual to successfully resist.

That they had one of the great thinkers of our time in their midst, the Viennese have never understood.

F.A. Hayek
Lisbon
May 1977

1

Historicism

The first source of my political and historical indoctrination was the *Gartenlaube*, the periodical of provincial Germany. In 1888, the year of the three kaisers, it ran numerous illustrated features on the lives of the two who had died. Not seven years old at the time, I devoured these articles with great fervor.

The historical bias of this family publication presented itself to me later and more explicitly in the works of the *kleindeutsch*[1] historicists. As an Austrian, it was not difficult for me to identify strong political overtones in their writings. I soon began to see through their methods of analysis, which had been unflatteringly referred to as falsifications of history. *Großdeutsch*[2] historicists

---

[1]The *Kleindeutsche Lösung* (literally "Small German Solution") was a nineteenth-century political idea espousing a unified Germany led by Hohenzollern Prussia, excluding the Austrian Empire.

[2]The idea of a *Großdeutschland* (a "Greater Germany") stood in contrast to that of the *Kleindeutsche Lösung*. The German parliament elected after the early successes of the revolution of 1848 was split between the two options, with the democratic left favoring a republican *Großdeutschland*,

were no more honest or thorough in their work; they were merely less competent.

Upon graduation from high school, the problems of economic, legal, administrative, and social history attracted me more than did those of political history. I decided to study law rather than history, which had been my earlier plan. At the time the study of law at Austrian universities was arranged in such a way that three to four semesters of the total eight were dedicated to the history of law exclusively, with the remaining four to five being relegated to political economy and public law. The school of law provided students with more favorable options in the study of history than did the school of liberal arts. The political historians who taught in the latter were scholars of third and fourth rank. The only historicist of significance coming out of Austria at the time was Heinrich Friedjung, who was denied access to an academic career, as the emphasis in historical education at the University of Vienna lay in the study of paleography.

In 1900, historicism stood at the zenith of its success. The historical method was considered the sole scientific method of the science of human action. From the height of historical enlightenment, the historical political economist looked down upon the orthodox dogmatist with unspeakable disdain. Economic history was the fashionable science, and, in the German-speaking world, Schmoller was considered the master of political economy. Ambitious young men from around the world flocked to his seminar.

I was still in high school when I became aware of a contradiction in the position assumed by those in Schmoller's circle. On the one hand they rejected the positivist demand for scientific

---

where as the liberal center favored a *Kleindeutschland* with a constitutional monarchy. In the end, the *Kleindeutsche Lösung* prevailed, but the Prussian king rejected the crown offered to him.

law built on a society's historical experience; on the other hand they were of the opinion that economic theory could be abstracted from a society's economic experience. It was astonishing to me that this inconsistency was hardly noticed.

The relativism of the school, which degenerated into many of its adherents' developing a blind adulation of the past and its institutions, also aroused my disapproval. Whereas some fanatics for progress had judged all that was old to be damnable and bad, these pseudohistorians rejected anything new in arduous preference for the old. At that time I had not yet come to comprehend the significance of liberalism, but the fact that it was an achievement not realized before the eighteenth century provided on its own no sufficient argument against it. I failed to understand attempts to justify tyranny, superstition, and intolerance through relativism and historicism. I considered attempts to uphold the sexual morality of the past as a model for the present a brazen falsification of history. But the most extreme excesses occurred in the areas of church and religious history, where both Catholics and Protestants tried to suppress everything they found to be disagreeable.

On at least one point, the honesty of Austrian legal historians' work stood in refreshing contrast to the bias found in the efforts of the Prussian historians. In his five-hour lecture on Austrian history, which was required of all first semester law students, Professor Siegmund Adler dealt with Duke Rudolf the Founder, and the forgery of the *Privilegium Majus*, with a thoroughness that could withstand the sharpest criticism. It was not until decades later that Ernst Karl Winter found the courage to palliate this chapter of Austrian history by labeling the late duke a socialist whose socialism exceeded even that of Kaiser Friedrich Wilhelm I, the idol of German socialists.

It was not clear to me that an argument against private property could be derived from the fact that a piece of land had, in the past, been considered community property; nor could I understand that monogamy and family should be abolished because of promiscuity that had existed in the past. I saw nothing but nonsense in these trains of thought.

Likewise, I failed to understand the contrasting point of view, which, characteristically enough was held by those same people. According to this opinion, any development made over time was progress, a higher development, and therefore morally justified.

The honest relativism of genuinely inquisitive historicists had nothing in common with the false relativism of this school. Logically, however, it was not more firmly founded. According to its tenets, there was no distinction between expedient and inexpedient politics. Dealing in a realm of givens, it remains to the sage historicist not to judge, but to observe and to accept, in much the same way that a natural scientist relates to natural phenomena.

It does not take many words to highlight the fallacy in this point of view, which divides many economists even today. Making value judgments is not the calling and task of science. But it is one of the two tasks of science, and, according to some, the only task of science, to instruct us with regard to the suitability of means used in attaining certain ends. The natural scientist does not make value judgments, but informs his fellow man as to what means are available to him for the purpose of reaching particular goals. It is up to the sciences of human action to examine the appropriateness of the means and methods used in the attainment of the action's objective, rather than to make judgments concerning the ultimate objective itself.

I discussed these matters frequently with Ludo Hartmann, and in later years with Max Weber and Alfred Frances Pribram. All three were so steeped in historicism that it was difficult for them to recognize that my position was correct. Fiery temperaments on the parts of Hartmann and Weber eventually won out over philosophical misgivings, thrusting them into lives of political action. Lacking in this urge toward action, Pribram remained faithful to his quietism and agnosticism. Of him one could say what Goethe said about the Sphinx:

Sitzen vor den Pyramiden
Zu der Völker Hochgericht,
Übershwemmungen, Krieg and Frieden
Und verziehen kein Gesicht.[3]

As for the *kleindeutsch* historicists, I found fault in their crude and materialistic position concerning power. In their view, power meant bayonets and cannons, and *Realpolitik* involved militarism. Anything else was called illusion, idealism, and utopianism. They were never able to comprehend Hume's famous teaching, namely, that all government is founded on public opinion.

In this respect, their great adversary, Heinrich Friedjung, was of the same thinking. A few months before the outbreak of the First World War, he told me,

> I do not understand what is said of the mood of the Russian masses, and the revolutionary ideologies that inspire the Russian intelligentsia. It is all so vague and unclear. Rather, it is the will of leading statesman and the plans they hammer out that are the deciding factors.

This was no different from the opinion of Johann Schober, the petty constable who later became Austria's chancellor. Toward the end of 1915 he reported to his superiors that he did not believe that the situation in Russia would result in revolution. "Who would lead this revolution? Certainly not that Mr. Trotsky, who takes care to sit in the Café Central and read newspapers."

---

[3] Sitting in front of the Pyramids,
In the people's highest court,
Floods and war and peace,
Without change in facial expression.

In 1900, there was only one man on the faculty in Vienna who belonged to the German Historical School. Karl Grünberg had worked with Knapp in Strasbourg, and then published a book that described the agrarian policies of the Austrian government in the *Sudetenland*. This book slavishly followed in form, presentation, and method Knapp's book on the old provinces of Prussia. It was neither economic history, nor was it administrative history. It was an excerpt from official documents, an account of policies as described in these documents. It could have been easily produced by any able government official.

It was Grünberg's ambition to create a center for economic history in Vienna, much as Knapp had done in Strasbourg. At the time, Knapp's students were researching peasant liberation in specific German provinces. For his own students, Grünberg was planning an account of peasant liberation in different regions of Austria. He arranged for me to work on the history of the landlord-peasant relationship in Galicia. I tried as best I could to free myself of too narrow an association with Knapp's system. I succeeded only in part, and my resulting 1902 publication was more a history of government measures than an economic history. A second historical work, which I published independently of Grünberg in 1905, was not much better; under its title, *Zur Geschichte der österreichischen Fabrikgesetzgebung*,[4] it described older Austrian laws regarding limitation of child labor in industry.

While dedicating a great deal of my time to these publications, I made plans for more extensive research. These would be social and economic histories, and not excerpts from official documents. These plans were never realized. After having completed my university studies, I was never again at leisure to spend time working in archives and libraries.

---

[4]"A Contribution to Austrian Factory Legislation."

It was because of my constant and burning interest in history that I was able to recognize the inadequacy of German historicism early on. This historicism did not deal with scientific problems; it dealt with the glorification and justification of Prussian policies and the Prussian authoritative government. German universities were state institutions, and their instructors were civil servants. Professors were aware of their status as servants of the Prussian king. If they used their nominal independence to criticize government measures, it had no meaning beyond that of the grumbling commonly associated with any such body of officials.

This university "enterprise" of economic political science was off-putting to young people of intelligence and genuine curiosity. In contrast, it held a strong attraction to halfwits. It was not difficult to walk into an archive and paste together a historical thesis from a stack of official reports. Before long, most university positions were held by men who could be classified as intellectually limited, were their abilities to be measured against those of men in independent professions. One must bear this in mind when wanting to understand how men such as Werner Sombart acquired such great reputations. Not being entirely stupid and uneducated had its merits.

University instruction in an *a priori* science presents special problems if we are to adhere to the principle that an instructor ought to be a researcher as well. In every field there are very few who can make actual contributions to its intellectual treasury. In the *a posteriori* sciences, however, pioneers and followers work together with the same tools, and there exists no outward distinction between them. In his laboratory, every professor of chemistry can compare himself with the great pioneer. Although his contribution may be modest, his research methods are the same.

Things are different in philosophy, in economics, and in a certain sense, in mathematics. If academic positions were contingent upon independent contributions to economics, barely a dozen professors could be found throughout the world. If positions are awarded only to those researchers who had made original contributions, care must be taken to take into account research done in related areas. In effect, this makes the appointment to academic positions dependent upon scholarly activity in other areas: the history of ideas and doctrine, history of economics, and especially the economic history of the most recent past, which is often erroneously labeled economic problems of the present.

The fiction perpetrated in scholarly circles that all professors are equal does not permit professors of economics to be divided into two classes: those who work independently as theorists, and those whose work consists of economic history and description. The inferiority complex of these "empiricists" has led to a campaign against theory.

It was in Germany (and later in other countries) that this campaign first took on a nationalist tone. In the first half of the nineteenth century, professors in Germany were at best mere transmitters of English economic thought. Only a few, among them Hermann and Mangoldt, earned places in the history of political economy. The older historical school maintained a nationalistic resentment toward western thought, and Nazi arguments rejecting western ideas were thrown into the mix by the younger historical school. University professors delighted in replacing bad English teachings with singularly beatific German ones. John Stuart Mill was the last Englishman with whom the Germans were somewhat familiar. He was the "epigone" of the evil classicists, and was given credit for having anticipated some of the great ideas of German economics.

The German Historical School did not produce a single thought. It did not write a single page in the history of science. For eighty years it eagerly propagandized for National Socialism, but the ideas for this propaganda were adopted, not created. The school's historical investigations were methodically deficient, and its publications were heavy handed at best. But the worst aspects of the school were its untruthfulness and conscious dishonesty. Writers of her partisan literature were always looking "up" for inspiration from government ministers, and professors did their best, despite their limitations, to serve their masters: first the Hohenzollern family; then the Marxists; and finally, Hitler. Werner Sombart lent shape to their ideas most pointedly upon designating Hitler as the bearer of divine mandate, since "all authority is from God."

The greatest achievement of historicism, the historical theory of the Southwest German School of philosophy, was the work of other men. Max Weber, the school's consummate scholar, spent a lifetime fighting against such German pseudohistoricism.

2
Etatism

By around 1900, most people in German-speaking countries were either etatists or state socialists. The dark episode of history known to us as capitalism had run its course once and for all. The future belonged to the state. The state would take over all enterprise suitable for nationalization and the rest would be regulated in a way that would prevent businessmen from exploiting workers and consumers. Since the fundamental laws of economics were as yet unknown, the problems presented by interventionism could not be seen. Had they been recognized, everyone would have opted for socialism. But without this knowledge it remained unclear if interventionism or state socialism was more desirable.

The program of the Marxist Social Democrats was much clearer. Marxists rejected interventionism theoretically as mere bourgeois reformism; in actuality, however, they freely promoted a theory of reformism that was all encompassing. Their work had long emphasized labor unions, thereby flouting doubts raised by Marx and his strictest disciples. Even so, they jealously guarded every bit of their master's orthodoxy. The party rejected Bernstein's attempt to revise the theory, which sought to lessen the glaring contradictions between Marxism and party policy. The victory of orthodoxy was not complete, however. A revisionist group did survive, and it found its expression in the *Socialist Monthly*.

Middle-class opposition to the Social Democratic Party was not aroused because of the party's economic program, but because of its simplistic description of extant institutions and its denegation of all facts that did not fit into its scheme. According to the latter, all evil in the world stemmed from capitalism and this evil would be eradicated through socialism. Alcoholism was caused by a free market for liquor, and a free armaments market was to blame for war. Prostitution existed only in capitalist societies, and religion was the clever invention of priests intended to render compliance from the proletariat. Capitalism alone caused scarcity of goods, whereas socialism would bring unknown wealth to all. Nothing, however, excited the opposition of the middle class more than the social-democratic program of free love.

And yet everyone found that the social-democratic program contained a kernel of truth. This was seen in the demand for social reform and a continued push toward socialization. The Marxist spirit animated all governments and political parties. They differed from the Social Democratic Party in that they did not take into consideration the state's expropriation of all owners and its purely bureaucratic management of all enterprise. Their socialism was not that of Lenin, who wanted to organize all industry according to the model of the state-run postal service. Theirs was a socialism that corresponded to the state-controlled economy of the Hindenburg program of the second period of the First World War, and the "German" socialism of Hitler. Private property and ownership should be formally retained, but business was to be managed according to government directives. Church socialists wanted to retain a preferred position for the Christian church; likewise, state socialists supported the monarchy and the army.

Upon entering the university, I too was an etatist, through and through. I differed from my fellow students, however, in that I was consciously anti-Marxist. At the time I knew little of Marx's writings, but was acquainted with most important works of Kautsky. I was an avid reader of the *Neue Zeit*, and had followed the revisionist debate with great attention. The platitudes of Marxist literature repelled me. I found Kautsky almost ridiculous. As I entered into a more detailed study of the most important works of Marx, Engels, and Lassalle, I was incited to contradiction on all sides. It seemed incomprehensible to me that this garbled Hegelianism could have such enormous influence. I realized only later that party Marxists fell into two categories: those who had never studied Marx at all and were acquainted with only a few of the better known passages from his books, and those who knew of Marx only from textbooks, or, as autodidacts, had read none of the world's literature beyond that of Marx. Max Adler, for example, belonged to the former group. His knowledge of Marx was limited to the few pages in which the "super structure theory" had been developed. Prominent among the latter group were the Eastern Europeans, who led Marxism's ideological charge.

I have encountered nearly all of the Marxian theorists in western and central Europe during the course of my life, and among them I've found but one man who rises above modest mediocrity. Otto Bauer was the son of a wealthy north Bohemian manufacturer. While at *Reichenberger Gymnasium*,[1]

[1]A *Gymnasium* in the German-speaking world is roughly equivalent to a high school in the United States in terms of the age range of its students. With its rigorous admissions policies, however, it is more academic in orientation.

he found himself under the influence of the same teacher who had introduced Heinrich Herkner to the ideas of social reform nearly two decades before.

Bauer came to the University of Vienna as a staunch Marxist. Equipped with untiring diligence and a glowing facility for ideas, he became conversant in German idealistic philosophy and classical economics. He had an unusually broad knowledge of history including that of Slavic and oriental nations. He was well versed in current research in the natural sciences, was an excellent speaker, and could quickly and easily familiarize himself with the most difficult of problems. He was not a born trailblazer, to be sure, and one could not expect him to come up with new theories or ideas. But had he not been a Marxist, he could have become a statesman.

As a young man, Otto Bauer had made up his mind never to be untrue to his Marxian convictions, never to make concessions to reformism or socialist revisionism, and never to become a Millerand or a Miquel. No one was to outclass him in his Marxian radicalism. He was later strengthened in his resolve by his wife Helene Gumplowicz. He remained faithful to his intentions until the winter of 1918/19. At that time I was successful in convincing the Bauers that the collapse of a Bolshevist experiment in Austria would be inevitable in a very short time, perhaps within days. The supply of food in Austria was dependent on imports made possible only by the relief assistance of former enemies. Vienna's food supply would not have lasted more than eight or ten days on any given day during the nine months following the armistice. The Allies could have forced a surrender of a Bolshevist regime in Vienna without lifting a finger. There were few who recognized the state of affairs clearly. People were so convinced of the inevitability of Bolshevism that their main concern was securing a favorable place for themselves in the new order. The Catholic Church and its followers, the Christian Social Party, were prepared to befriend the Bolshevists with the same eagerness with which the bishops and archbishops would embrace National Socialism twenty years later. Bank directors and industrialists hoped to make good livings as managers under the Bolshevists. A certain Mr. Guenther, an industrial consultant to the *Bodenkreditanstalt*,[2] assured Otto Bauer, in my presence, that he would prefer serving the people to serving a group of stockholders. The effect of this kind of declaration can be appreciated when one understands that this man was considered, although mistakenly, the best industrial manager in Austria.

I knew what was at stake. Bolshevism would lead Vienna to starvation and terror within a few days. Plundering hordes would take to the streets and a second blood bath would destroy what was left of Viennese culture. After discussing these problems with the Bauers over the course of many evenings, I was finally able to persuade them of my view. Bauer's resulting moderation was a determining factor in Vienna's fate.

Bauer was too intelligent not to realize that I had been right, but he never forgave me for having turned him into a Millerand. The attacks of his fellow Bolshevists hit close to home. But he directed his animosity toward me instead of toward his opponents. A powerful loather, he opted for ignoble means to destroy me. He tried to cause the nationalistic students and professors at the University of Vienna to turn against me. The attempt failed. I have not spoken with the Bauers since. I had always held Bauer's character in an unwarranted high esteem, by the way. When, during the civil unrest of February 1934, Secretary Fay announced on the radio that Otto Bauer had deserted the fighting workers and fled abroad with party funds, I considered the

---

[2]*Bodenkreditanstalt* translates literally into "land bank." The *Bodenkreditanstalt* began as a privileged bank in the Austrian mortgage market, but also turned to industrial investments and eventually functioned as a vehicle for a semi-public industrial policy. It was the most powerful bank in Austria with very large holdings in almost all sectors of industry. It went bankrupt in September of 1929.

statement slanderous. I would have not believed Bauer capable of such cowardice.

During my first two semesters as a university student I belonged to the *Sozialwissenschaftlicher Bildungsverein*,[3] an organization serving students interested in the problems of economics and society, as well as older gentlemen who valued the association with students. Michael Hainisch, who later became President of Austria, was chairman at the time, and membership reflected all political parties. Among Social Democratic leaders, Karl Renner took a special interest in the association. Historians Ludo Hartmann and Kurt Kaser were frequently found at the discussions. Two of the student members most vivid in my memory are Otto Weininger and Friedrich Otto Hertz. My interest began to slacken during my third semester. I found that too much time could be lost on activities associated with the group.

I had thrown myself into the study of economics and social politics with great enthusiasm. At first I devoured the writings of the social reformers without much criticism. If a sociopolitical measure did not produce the desired result, this could only have been because it was not radical enough. In liberalism, which rejected social reform, I recognized the vestiges of a worldview that merited spirited opposition.

It was during my fifth semester at the university that I first began to entertain doubts concerning the supremacy of interventionism. Professor Philippovich assigned me to do an investigation of housing conditions. The following semester, Professor Löffler, in his seminar on criminal law, asked me to research changes in law affecting domestic servants, who at the time were still subject to the corporal punishment of their employers. It became obvious to me that any improvement in the plight of the working classes was a result of capitalism, and that the outcome of

---

[3]Association for Education in the Social Sciences.

social legislation often ran opposite to the intentions of its authors.

It was the study of political economy, however, that led me to an understanding of the true nature of interventionism.

In 1908 I joined the *Zentralstelle für Wohnungsreform*,[4] a group who sought to improve unsatisfactory housing conditions throughout Austria. I was quickly named as a consultant on pending real estate tax reform, a successor to Professor Robert Mayer who had been appointed to the position of minister of finance.

Taxation that discouraged large capital investment and entrepreneurship in the housing sector was the cause of these undesirable housing conditions. Austria was a country without beneficial real estate speculation. Exorbitant taxation of corporations and high tax rates on capital gains prevented those with capital from entering the housing market. In order to provide relief, one would have to reduce taxes on corporations and capital gains. There was no inclination to take this direction; hatred of large-scale capital and speculation were deeply ingrained.

Tax rates on returns from real estate were also exceedingly high. In Vienna, more than 40 percent of the gross revenue was claimed and collected in the form of federal, state, and local taxes. Homeowners and building contractors were up in arms. They considered these taxes solely to blame for high rents. Most homeowners were small businessmen whose savings were invested in houses financed at 50 percent of their customarily overappraised value. Building contractors, lacking in capital, worked to fill the orders of this clientele or worked at their own expense, hoping to sell homes as soon as they were completed. Both groups, homeowners and contractors, had great political

[4]Central Association for Housing Reform.

influence through which they hoped to achieve a considerable reduction in mortgage rates.

A reduction of taxes on existing housing and land returns had not reduced rents, and had, in fact, raised returns and market prices accordingly. In order to make up for lost revenue, the government had to seek other tax income as a substitute. Such reform called for the imposition of new taxes to compensate for tax reductions to landlords.

Receiving general acknowledgment of my views was not easy. My appraisal of the situation was met by the misgivings of those in the Central Association at first. But complete success soon followed.

My activity with the *Zentralstelle*, which remained intense until the outbreak of the war, brought me great satisfaction. In addition to Robert Mayer, many outstanding economists worked there: the brothers Karl and Ewald Pribram, Emil von Fürth, Paul Schwarz, Emil Perels, and Rudolf Maresch.

I was in constant disagreement with my colleagues on just one point. The *Zentralstelle* had connections with the *Kaiser Franz Joseph Jubiläum-Stiftung-für Volkswohnungen*,[5] which was endowed with large funds to finance housing in general. The same funds also financed the construction of two housing projects for single men. I found the latter to be superfluous. Young men in lower-income brackets customarily boarded with families. It was believed, however, that arrangements of this nature posed a threat to morality. Because of my experience doing investigations as a field worker for Löffler and Philippovich, I was of a different opinion. Intimate liaisons did on occasion develop in these boarding houses; the normal result, however, was a marriage contract. In fact, a probe initiated by the Viennese vice squad revealed that very few young women living

[5]Kaiser Franz Joseph Anniversary Foundation for Public Housing.

under supervision in these houses declared boarders or "sleepers" to be their first seducers. In contrast, an experienced adviser to the police considered houses for single men breeding grounds for homosexuality. It was on these grounds that I could not support their funding.

My view did not prevail. But the outcome of the discussion was of little consequence, as the war halted further construction of such buildings. Adolf Hitler was living in one at the time.

3

The Austrian Problem

The multilingual Hapsburg state could have made itself indispensable to the grand design. It could have created a constitution that enabled people of different tongues to live peacefully under one commonwealth. Perthaler's constitution of 1867 was an attempt at just that, but it was destined for failure. The Sudetenland's barons and their dominant party fought liberalism with all means at their disposal.

In 1900, Austria was an entity unwanted by its subjects. The nationality principle[1] denied the state its justification for existence, and everyone was counting on its forthcoming dissolution.

It was only in Vienna that there was still a small number of people who concerned themselves with methods of preserving the state. The destruction of the Hapsburg monarchy and the events it triggered later revealed that these men took pains to

[1]The nationality principle, and moreover, the word "national," within this chapter, make reference to linguistic or subpolitical groups, and stand in contrast to Austria-Hungary as a unified state.

save Europe and all of civilization from great catastrophe. But lacking in any sustainable ideological base, their efforts were destined to be in vain.

This lack was clearly seen in no one's wanting to allow for sincerity on the part of those who had Austria's future at heart. One was permitted to be a "good" German; that is, a nationalistic German, Czech, or Pole, or the like. One could be, for example, a German cleric or a Bohemian landowner and be colorless, linguistically speaking, yet look out for the interests of one's own region or social class alone. But he who thought as an Austrian was considered someone who only wanted to endear himself to the powers that be. In reality, the "crown" did not give preference to such strident loyalists; it favored "moderate" irredentists.

No one in Vienna was able to avoid concern with the problems of nationalism during this period. Otto Bauer and Karl Renner first presented their ideas promoting a program of national autonomy, which later appeared in book form, within the context of the *Sozialwissenschaftlichen Bildungsverein*.[2] Ludo Hartmann also reported on his investigations into the problems of linguistic assimilation, but these, unfortunately, were never published. Professor of public law, Adolf Bernatzik, steered my attention toward the problem of the "national land registry," which was to yield the basis for uniform election standards.

I tracked all of these efforts with great interest, but I had my doubts as to their potential for success. It was not to be denied that the peoples of the *Donaumonarchie*[3] wanted to see its destruction. Was defending a state run by frivolous, uneducated counts and ambitious but characterless civil servants really worth the effort? Events leading to the downfall of the Koerber administration made a deep impression on all of those concerned with

---

[2]Association for Education in the Social Sciences.

[3]"Danube Monarchy." Mises is referring to Austria-Hungary.

the preservation of the state. Among the many prime ministers who governed the old Austria during its last twenty-five years, Ernest von Koerber was the only one who pursued policies to that end. Rudolf Sieghart, his brilliant and gifted senior cabinet member, supported his efforts; Böhm-Bawerk was his minister of finance. Koerber had instructed his district attorneys to adopt a policy of leniency when it came to shutting down newspapers. Thus it happened that when one of Vienna's German nationalist papers published an article denigrating the Sacrament of the Altar, the article went unchallenged. Opponents of Koerber seized the opportunity to topple his administration: confessors and ladies at the court of the Arch Duchess busied themselves feverishly with denouncing the "Jew" Koerber (one of his grandmothers or great grandmothers had been Jewish) as a desecrator of the Church. In so doing, the last man genuinely concerned with the continuation of the state was forced out of office.

I must admit now that I judged the shortcomings of Austrian affairs too severely at the time, and that conditions abroad, which I knew only from books or short, superficial visits, appeared to me in too rosy a light. But this did not change the facts. The Hapsburg state, lacking an ideological basis of national unity, could not cope with the same degree of political mismanagement that seemed reasonable for other countries. Errors endurable by others could prove fatal to Austria. Faulty politics would undo her more quickly than it would English or French states.

The fact that state and national lines did not overlap in Austria prompted the study of problems that were not readily observable in other countries. The English and French languages are to this day lacking in expressions that make possible a correct representation of the economic and political problems that arise from such dualism.

I thereby concerned myself primarily with the consequences of interventionism. Each individual interventionist measure would affect the balance of power in a nationally mixed state.

Austrian politicians were acutely aware of this, and the minutes of parliamentary proceedings as well as the press were rich with material on the matter. I recognized the full scope of these problems for the first time when I became a member of the *Handelspolitischen Zentralstelle*[4] in the *Viennese Handelskammer*[5] in 1909.

My plan was to investigate these problems in great detail. I conducted my first university seminar during the academic year 1913–1914, and selected four young scholars to do research on the position of Germans, Czechs, Poles, and Hungarians with regard to the foreign trade policies of the Austro-Hungarian customs union. With these policies, the Hungarian government and the autonomous provincial governments sought measures to create administrative protection benefiting their respective nationals. I hoped to find a fifth collaborator who would concentrate on the Italian position. I, myself, wanted to write a comprehensive report that would be published along with the work of my colleagues.

Of the four young scholars, two fell during the early weeks of the war. A third was reported missing in action in the Carpathian Mountains during the winter of 1914–1915. The fourth was taken prisoner by the Russians at Volhynia in July of 1916. He was never heard from again.

[4]Central Committee on Trade Policy.

[5]Chamber of Commerce.

4

The Austrian School of Economics

When I first came to the university, Carl Menger was nearing the end of his teaching career. There was little attention paid the Austrian School of economics at the university, and I had no interest in it at the time.

Around Christmas, 1903, I read Menger's *Grundsätze der Volkswirtschaftslehre*[1] for the first time. It was through this book that I became an economist.

Many years passed before I encountered Carl Menger in person. When I met him he was already over seventy years old, hard of hearing, and plagued by an eye disorder. His mind, however, was young and vigorous. I have asked myself again and again why this man did not make better use of his last decades. That he could still do brilliant work was evidenced by his essay, "Geld,"[2] which he contributed to the *Handwörterbuch der Staatswissenschaften*.[3]

---

[1]*Principles of Economics* (1871).

[2]"Money."

[3]*Encyclopedia of State Sciences*.

I believe I know the cause of Menger's discouragement and premature silence. His keen intellect had recognized in which direction Austria, Europe, and the world were pointed; he saw this greatest and highest of all civilizations rushing toward the abyss. He had anticipated the atrocities with which we are faced today; he knew the consequences of the world's turning away from liberalism and capitalism, and had done what he could to battle these trends. His book, *Untersuchungen über die Methode der Sozialwissenschaften*,[4] was intended as a polemic effort to counter the destructive intellectual currents with which Prussian universities were poisoning the world. He realized that his fight was futile and hopeless, and became filled with a dark pessimism that exhausted his strength. He passed this pessimism on to his student and friend, Rudolf, successor to the throne. The crown prince took his own life because of despair over the future of his empire and that of European civilization, not because of a woman. The young girl had had a death wish of her own and he took her into death with him; he did not commit suicide on her account.

My grandfather had a brother who died many years before I was born. This brother, Dr. Joachim Landau, was a liberal member of the Austrian Parliament and a close friend of his party colleague, Dr. Max Menger, brother of Carl Menger. One day he told my grandfather about a conversation he had had with Carl Menger.

According to my grandfather, as told to me around 1910, Carl Menger had made the following remarks:

The policies being pursued by the European powers will lead to a terrible war ending with gruesome revolutions, the extinction of European culture and destruction of prosperity for people of all nations. In anticipation of these inevitable events,

---

[4]*Untersuchungen über die Methode der Sozialwissenschaften und der politischen Okonomie insbesondere* (Investigations into the Method of the Social Sciences with Special Reference to Economics).

all that can be recommended are investments in gold hoards and the securities of the two Scandinavian countries.

Menger's savings, in fact, were invested in Swedish securities.

One who so clearly foresees disaster and the destruction of everything he deems valuable before his fortieth year cannot avoid pessimism and depression. Ancient rhetoricians were careful to consider the kind of life King Priam would have had, had he at the age of twenty already foreseen the fall of Ilium![5] Carl Menger barely had the first half of his life behind him when he recognized the inevitability of the demise of his own Troy.

This same pessimism consumed all sharp-sighted Austrians. The tragic privilege attached to being Austrian was the opportunity it afforded to recognize fate. Grillparzer's melancholy and peevishness arose from this source. The feeling of being powerless in the face of impending disaster drove the purist and most able of patriots, Adolf Fischof, into isolation.

It is understandable that I discussed Knapp's *Staatliche Theorie des Geldes*[6] with Menger frequently.

"It is," said Menger,

> the logical development of Prussian police science. What should one make of a nation whose elite, after two hundred years of economics, admire such nonsense and perceive it as an epiphany, when in fact it isn't even new? What can one expect of such a people?

Menger's successor at the University of Vienna was Friedrich von Wieser. Wieser was an honest scholar, and a man of high personal cultivation and refined intellect. He had the good fortune of becoming acquainted with Menger's work earlier than others, and it is to his credit that he recognized its significance. He added to the discipline in certain respects, but

---

[5]The ancient city of Troy.

[6]*The State Theory of Money*. Knapp claimed that money was in its origin and its essence a pure creature of the state.

he was not an original thinker, and probably did more harm than good overall. He never really grasped the core of subjectivism, a limitation that caused him to make many unfortunate mistakes. His imputation theory is untenable. His ideas on value calculation support the claim that he cannot be called a member of the Austrian School. He had more in common with those of the Lausanne School, two brilliant representatives of which were found in Austria in Rudolph Auspitz and Richard Lieben.

What distinguishes the Austrian School and will lend it everlasting fame is its doctrine of economic action, in contrast to one of economic equilibrium or nonaction. The Austrian School makes use of the ideas of rest and equilibrium, without which economic thought cannot get along. But it is always aware of the purely instrumental nature of these ideas. The Austrian School aims to account for prices actually paid in the market, and not just prices that might be paid under certain never-realizable conditions. It rejects the mathematical method, not because of ignorance or an aversion to mathematical accuracy, but because it does not place importance upon the detailed description of the condition of a hypothetical and static equilibrium. The Austrian School has never succumbed to the fatal illusion that values can be measured, and has never misunderstood that statistical data has nothing to do with economic theory, but belongs to the history of economics alone.

Because Austrian economics is a discipline that concerns human action, even Schumpeter cannot be counted among the school's ranks. In his first books, Schumpeter aligns himself with Wieser and Walras but not with Menger and Böhm-Bawerk. To him, economics is a discipline of "economic quantities" and not one of human action. His *Theory of Economic Development*[7] is a typical product of this equilibrium theory.

[7] *Theorie der wirtschaftlichen Entwicklung.*

It is necessary to correct the misunderstandings that can be called forth by using the expression "Austrian School." Neither Menger nor Böhm-Bawerk wanted to found a school in the sense customarily used in university circles. They never attempted to turn young students into blind disciples, nor did they, in turn, provide these same students with professorships. They knew that through books and an academic course of instruction they could promote an understanding suited to dealing with economic problems, thus rendering an important service to society. They understood, however, that they could not rear economists. As pioneers and creative thinkers, they recognized that one cannot arrange for scientific progress, nor breed innovation according to plan. They never attempted to propagandize their theories. Truth would prevail of its own accord when man possessed the faculties necessary to perceive it. Using impertinent means to cause people to pay lip service to a teaching was of no use if they lacked the ability to grasp its substance and significance.

Menger made no efforts to extend favors to colleagues that would be reciprocated with recommendations for appointments. As minister and then ex-minister of finance, Böhm-Bawerk could have used his influence; he always spurned such behavior. Menger did make occasional attempts, without success, to prevent the promotion of those, for example, Zweideneck, who had no sense of what was going on in economics. Böhm-Bawerk made no such attempts. In fact, he advanced rather than hindered the appointments of Professors Gottl and Spann at the *Brünner Technische Hochschule.*[8]

Menger's position on such questions is best illustrated by a note discovered by Hayek while perusing Menger's scientific papers. It reads, "In science, there is only one sure method for

[8]Brno University of Technology.

the ultimate triumph of an idea: one should allow any contrary notion to run its course completely." Schmoller, Bücher, and Lujo Brentano thought differently. They denied the opportunity to teach at German universities to those who did not follow them blindly.

Faculty positions at Austrian universities thus fell into the hands of the heirs of German historicism. Alfred Weber and Spiethoff, were, in turn, vested with a position at the University of Prague. A certain Professor Günther became professor of economics at Innsbruck. I mention all of this only to cast the claim of Franz Oppenheimer in proper light, namely, that the school of marginal utility monopolized the teaching of economic theory. Schumpeter was full professor in Bonn for many years. This was the only case in which a German university had appointed a teacher who belonged to the field of modern economics. Among the many hundreds of men who taught economics at German universities between 1870 and 1934, not one could be found who was acquainted with the works of the Austrian, Lausanne, or modern Anglo-Saxon schools. A *Privatdozent*[9] would never be promoted to the faculty were he suspected of belonging to one of these schools. Knies and Dietzel were the last economists on German faculties. In the German Empire they did not teach economics, but Marxism or Nazism. The same was true in Czarist Russia, where "legal" Marxism or economic history was taught in place of economics. The fact that professors and lecturers in Austria were allowed to teach economics was incompatible with the totalitarian claim of German "economic state sciences."

The Austrian School of economics was Austrian in the sense that it emerged from the soil of an Austrian culture that National Socialism would trample down. In this soil, Franz Brentano's philosophy could take root. In this soil, Bolzano's epistemology, Mach's empiricism, Husserl's phenomenology,

---

[9]Unsalaried lecturer.

and Breuer's and Freud's psychoanalysis reached maturity. The air in Austria was free of the specter of Hegelian dialectics. In Austria, one did not feel it was his national duty to "overcome" the ideas of Western Europe. In Austria, eudaemonism, hedonism, and utilitarianism were not precluded, but studied.

It would be a mistake to assume that the Austrian government promoted all of these great movements. On the contrary, it withdrew the teaching assignments of Bolzano and Brentano; it isolated Mach, and did not bother at all with Husserl, Breuer, and Freud. It valued the competent official in Böhm-Bawerk, not the economist.

Böhm was a professor in Innsbruck. He grew weary of this position; the intellectual desert of this university, the city, and the province of Tirol became unbearable for him. He preferred employment in Vienna's ministry of finance. He was offered a gainful pension when he finally retired from government service, but this he rejected and requested a professorship at the University of Vienna.

The opening of Böhm-Bawerk's seminar was a great day in the history of the University of Vienna and in the development of economics. Böhm chose the fundamentals of the theory of value as the theme of the first semester; Otto Bauer sought to pick apart the subjectivism of value theory from a Marxist point of view. The discussion between Bauer and Böhm filled the entire winter semester while other participants remained in the background. Bauer's brilliant gift was on display; he proved himself to be a worthy opponent of the great master, whose critique of Marxian economics had dealt it a fatal blow. I believe that in the end even Bauer himself had to admit to the unsustainability of the Marxian labor theory of value. He abandoned his intention to write a reply to Böhm's critique of Marx. The first volume in this series on Marxian theory yielded a sensation-causing rejoinder from Hilferding. Bauer openly admitted to me that Hilferding did not grasp the problems at hand.

I took part in Böhm's seminar regularly until I was promoted in 1913. During the last two winter semesters in which I still attended the seminar, discussions were dedicated to my theory of money and credit: my explanation of money's purchasing was dealt with in the first; the second focused on my business cycle theory. The difference of opinion that emerged between Böhm and me on these points will be addressed later.

Böhm was a brilliant seminar leader. He considered himself more of a chairman than a teacher, and would enter into the debate on occasion. Unfortunately, babblers sometimes abused the freedom to speak that was allowed participants. Especially disruptive was the nonsense that Otto Neurath asserted with fanatical force. The sharper wielding of a chairman's upper hand could have often proven beneficial, but Böhm wanted no part in this. His thinking was in line with that of Menger, who believed that in science everyone must be allowed to speak.

The lifework of Böhm-Bawerk lies before us in splendid proximity. His masterful critique of old economics and his own theories have become our prized possessions. And yet, one can assert that Böhm could have produced even more had the circumstances allowed for it. He developed thoughts in seminar lectures and personal conversations that far exceeded those contained in his writings. But his physical constitution could not withstand the planning of grand and new undertakings. His nerves were no longer suited to hard work. Even the two-hour seminar had its effects. It was only through the greatest ordering of daily habits that he could muster the strength he needed for science. His entire endeavor belonged to economics; relaxation and enjoyment were found in symphony concerts.

Worries over Austria's future and its culture darkened the evening of Böhm-Bawerk's life. He suffered a heart attack a few weeks after the outbreak of the war. My unit was stationed at the vanguard, east of Trampol. I was handed a newspaper carrying his obituary upon returning from patrol duty one evening early in September.

5

First Writings on the Theory of Money

Karl Helfferich, in his 1903 book, *Das Geld*, asserted that the theory of marginal utility had failed to solve the problem of money value. I wanted to investigate the validity of this objection. In 1906 I began addressing the problems of money and banking, zealously studying the great theoretical works as well as the history of currencies in European countries, the United States, and British India. I sought to negotiate my way through an abundance of literature.

My first effort appeared in volume XVI of the *Zeitschrift für Volkswirtschaft, Sozialpolitik und Verwaltung*, under the title "Die Wirtschaftspolitischen Motive der Österreichischen Valutaregulierung."[1]

---

[1]*Journal for Economics, Social, and Policy Administration,* "The Economic Motives of Austrian Foreign Exchange Controls." No English translation of this was ever published.

In the fall of 1908, Edgeworth[2] asked Philippovich[3] if he wanted to write a short essay for the *Economic Journal*. It was to be no more than ten pages in length, and was to be a comprehensive look at the foreign-exchange policy of the *Österreichisch-Ungarischen Bank*.[4] Philippovich turned down the offer, but recommended me. I accepted, but decided to complete a full treatment of the subject in the German language as well. The resulting essay, "Das Problem gesetzlicher Aufnahme der Barzahlung in Österreich-Ungarn,"[5] appeared in Schmoller's *Jahrbuch* of 1909 and provoked strident protest from the most powerful members of the Austrian inflation party.

Ideas I pondered during the period in which I was writing these essays had already led me to a realization of the greatest failings of the prevailing monetary theory. I was convinced of the lack of validity of the balance-of-payments theory and the doctrine of "elasticity" of bank credit, but brief essays dealing with problems found in economic history and policy offer little opportunity for analysis of such large questions. I would have to save these efforts for the theoretical work I had planned for later, and, for the time being, maneuver within the framework of more widely accepted views.

I've chosen at this writing to bypass my critique of Knapp's treatment of the foreign exchange policies of central banks. Although admired by everyone in Germany and Eastern Europe during their day, his teachings have long been forgotten. But anyone who studies the general decline of German thought, and

---

[2]Francis Ysidro Edgeworth (Ysidro Francis Edgeworth) February 8, 1845–February 13, 1926.

[3]Eugen Philippovich von Philippsberg (1858–1917); economics and seminar leader.

[4]Austro-Hungarian Central Bank.

[5]"The Problem of the Legal Resumption of Gold Payments in Austria-Hungary."

in particular, that of German economic thought will find the most remarkable and psychologically interesting problems in those parts of Knapp's teachings that I criticize in the sixth part of my essay on cash payments. Knapp spoke of losses, for example, that the central bank suffered through foreign-exchange policy, and urged the state to reimburse the bank for these losses. One look at the bank's balance sheets and income statements could have shown him that foreign exchange transactions yielded the bank considerable profits, and that the state was in part responsible for these gains.

My essay dealt with the question of the legal requirement demanding the redemption of the Austro-Hungarian central bank's gold notes. For many years and without hesitation or discrimination, the bank had met all demands for foreign exchange at a rate that in no case exceeded the lawful gold parity of the crown by more than a margin. In gold-standard countries this is referred to as the upper gold point. In essence, gold payments in Austria-Hungary had resumed *de facto*. Under discussion now was whether this *de facto* situation should be made a legal requirement. One argument *for* the change was the more favorable conditions under which foreign markets would grant loans in Austrian currency, if gold payments for notes were independent of the bank's discretion. This position was championed in Hungary, especially, where the dismissive attitude of bank officials in some Austrian circles was seen as an effort to make Hungary dependent on Viennese money markets, and to make it impossible for it to tap cheaper money sources in other western countries. There were no cogent arguments *against* the legalization of the *de facto* situation.

Those opposed to the legally required resumption of gold payments had crafted an untenable theory to support their point of view. They argued that a bank that is legally obligated to make gold payments must adjust its rates to conform to the prevailing rate in the world market. They claimed that the Austro-Hungarian Bank found itself in a more favorable position due to the circumstances of not being obliged to make gold payments. The bank was in a position to differentiate between legitimate and illegitimate demand. Demand was said to be illegitimate if it aimed at shifting funds abroad in order to take advantage of higher interest rates abroad. The bank ought not consider this illegitimate interest-rate arbitrage, and only satisfy legitimate demand. In this way it could avoid, or at least postpone, the raising of rates made inevitable by mandatory redemption.

This doctrine was completely erroneous. The bank had never distinguished between legitimate and illegitimate demand; it had met all demands for payment since 1900. Had it gone ahead in the manner prescribed by those opposed to mandatory payments, all arbitrage speculators denied payment would have sought to buy foreign exchange in the open market. This would have raised the exchange rate and depreciated Austrian currency.

This doctrine was neither new nor uniquely Austrian. It was the old fallacy expounded by proponents of the French gold-premium policy fifteen or twenty years earlier. But these proponents never argued that such a policy would cause exchange rates to rise. They recommended this policy for France, one of the great exporters of capital at the time, and not for import countries such as Austria-Hungary. For a debtor country to loosen its relationship with foreign money markets would lead to an increase in the cost of its credits, not a reduction.

I had just completed my essay when I was surprised by an invitation from the vice president of the bank. I called on Mr. Waldmayer in his office. He said that he had heard from Professor Landesberger that I was in need of material for a study of bank policy, and that he would make it available to me. Of course I would be required to show my work to bank officials before it could go to press. I declined, politely, but decidedly. At the time I was not acquainted with Professor Landesberger, but knew that he was a good friend of Philippovich; I could only guess that Philippovich had granted him a look at my essay, or had told him of its contents.

From the conversation I had with Mr. Waldmayer, I was given the impression that bank management was especially interested in upholding existing conditions. This I could not understand. I knew that a mandatory gold payment would curtail the bank's right to invest some reserves in foreign accounts and obligations yielding interest, and that this would reduce the bank's gross returns. This would cause difficulty for stockholders above all, and for the two countries sharing in the bank's returns. Through appropriate changes to tax law, the secretaries of both treasuries would have seen to it that the greatest loss would have fallen on the stockholders. The interest of stockholders was represented by no one, least of all by the bank management, who had been appointed by the two governments. When I left Mr. Waldmayer's office I sensed that I would have been offered a considerable sum of money had I only been less dismissive. The bank maintained a press fund for such purposes.

It was many years later that an explanation was granted to me. In 1912, when I published an article on the fourth renewal of the bank's privileges, and was again attacked by the opponents of gold payments, Böhm-Bawerk instructed me in the causes of the bank's resistance. A portion of the proceeds from the obligations invested abroad, he reported, was credited to a special, secret account, which was at the disposal of the bank's governor alone. Already highly compensated bank officials, government officials who supervised the bank, journalists, politicians, and others received attractive payments from this secret fund on occasion. Böhm-Bawerk had learned about the fund by chance when the Hungarian finance minister complained that the share going to Austrians was too large compared to that going to Hungarians. The whole affair pained him to the highest degree, and caused him to loathe his position as well any other within the administration. But his wish to put and end to the antics was resisted by the Hungarian finance minister. "I feel obligated to make these facts known to you, in order that you may understand the background of the current struggle," Böhm remarked to me. I had to promise him that I would remain silent about the matter unless I should hear about it from other sources. I've remained silent until today, although the former press secretary of the bank told me most openly about the use of the fund a few years after the war. The actual amounts were more modest than those of Bismarck's famed *Reptilienfonds*.[6] They were nevertheless ample enough to explain strong opposition on the part of the bank's management and others to a reform that would have caused the source of the fund to run dry.

The strongest attacks against my argument came from Walther Federn, the publisher of a weekly economic journal, the *Österreichischen Volkswirt*.[7] Federn had held many lesser positions in banks, and had become the stock exchange reporter for various papers. He had been publishing the *Volkswirt* for some years, as it was financed by a bank director friend of his who went by the name of Rosenbaum. Federn was ignorant of economics, and with the exception of Knapp's *Staatliche Theorie des Geldes*, had never read a book on the subject. He possessed limited knowledge of economic conditions and statistics, and was wholly uncritical and incapable of independent thought. Though he himself was considered intellectually inept, his flowing style received praise. The principal source of revenue for his paper, which at the time had few subscribers, were the cash contributions which banks and large corporations paid newspapers and weekly and monthly journals for running advertisements, income statements, balance sheets, and announcements of stockholder meetings. No special conditions were attached to

---

[6]German Chancellor, Otto von Bismarck (1815–1898) used money confiscated from the exiled king of Hanover to create a secret fund for bribing reporters and bankrolling political movements in Germany and abroad. He called it the "Reptile Fund" because of his contempt for those who took such money.

[7]Austrian Economist.

the granting of these sums. Publishers naturally feared an interruption of further contributions on the part of concerns against which they had launched particularly nasty attacks, but moderate criticism of such enterprise was permissible.

It was not these contributions that robbed Viennese economic journalism of its independence. It was ignorance that fettered journalists. The great age of Viennese economic journalism had long since passed. That group of outstanding economists who had collaborated from 1860 to 1900—Menger among them—found no worthy heirs. The editorial staffs of the *Der Neue Freie Presse* and the *Neues Wiener Tagblatt* were the only ones composed of economists exhibiting knowledge and intellectual power. Other editors were ignorant and could not think; they depended on information coming from interested parties. Stock exchange reporters received their information from stock exchange men from the big banks. When a government regulation was passed or important business was transacted, journalists would rush to the responsible government officials or concerned business parties. The information the journalists received from them was then passed on to the public. The government did not need to bribe journalists; it was enough to merely inform them. Journalists feared nothing more than being made privy to information one day later than another member of the press. To avoid this plight, they were always prepared to represent the government's point of view. Their ignorance of economics afforded them the advantage of being able to proceed in a manner void of *sacrificium intellectus*.[8]

Federn had received a brushing up on the problems of foreign exchange by bank officials about two years before the publication of my essay; he published what he had learned in several articles in Viennese newspapers and in the *Frankfurter Zeitung*. He was very proud of his work, and considered it a

[8]Sacrifice of the intellect.

great journalistic achievement. My critique bruised his vanity. The fanatical intensity of his attacks had to do with this fact above all. Naturally, his desire to please bank officials and the treasury also played a role. Federn did not propagate the bank's position because of the sums it was paying to him, however. I am convinced as well that he did not know that such subsidies were coming from a secret fund that would have been placed into jeopardy by the legalization of gold payments. Individual beneficiaries could receive bank moneys in good faith: the bank also used funds derived from open revenues. Those who did not know the total amount spent on the press and other protected parties could assume that the endowment of the press fund was legal.

When Böhm-Bawerk revealed to me the secret of the bank's special fund, I was faced with a new problem. At this point I had been established, so to speak, for many years. I had worked in the treasury and in the office of the public prosecutor for many months; I had worked in the court for two years, and had been with the *Handelskammer* since 1909. I recognized the corruption that is an inevitable concomitant of interventionism; I knew very well that it extended to the highest positions of the state. But it was the first time that I faced opponents whose motives were not objective within the context of a scientific exchange. After long and in-depth consideration of what position I best take, I at last arrived at a clear response.

The economist must deal with doctrines, and not with men. It is for him to critique errant doctrine; it is not his charge to uncover the personal motives behind heterodoxy. The economist must face his opponents under the fictitious assumption that they are guided by objective considerations alone. It is irrelevant whether the advocate of a false notion acts in good or bad faith; what matters is if the stated notion is true or false. It is the charge of others to reveal corruption and enlighten the public concerning the same.

I have held fast to these principles throughout my life. Though I have known much, if not all, about the corruption of the interventionists and socialists with whom I have had to deal, I have never made use of this information. My point of view has not always been understood. Being the subject of the less than tasteful attacks of the Viennese Social Democrats, people have supplied me with ample material on the corrupt practices of these socialist leaders. Yet even without the help of informers I was well schooled in the moral decadence of the party; the materials passed on to me would not have been necessary had I wanted to occupy myself with the business of disclosure. The fact of my having graciously declined offers to prove fraud and embezzlement on the part of my opponents, admissible in courts of law, has often stirred resentment.

In the winter of 1912–1913, in the midst of the crisis created by the Balkan War, the Austro-Hungarian bank did indeed make an attempt to allow a portion of the demand for foreign exchange to remain unmet. The natural outcome of this was an increased demand on the open market and a climb in foreign exchange rates. The bank had to return at once to its former policy of unlimited and unconditional sale of foreign exchange. The bank imagined its operation of increasing just slightly the rate at which it was willing to sell to be an especially clever one. But all this action reaped was a decline in confidence in Austrian currency and the withdrawal of sizeable sums of foreign short-term money invested in Austria.

The intended goal of inflationists was the reduction of the purchasing power of the Austrian crown relative to gold, foreign exchange, and international economic goods. This was readily acknowledged by intelligent opponents of gold payment, such as Professor Landesberger and Richard Riedl, chairman of the Commerce Department's tariff division. Only a mental midget like Federn could believe that a refusal of note redemption would not affect the stability of exchange rates. Inflationists welcomed a small devaluation of the crown as a first step on a path that they considered to be a good one. Their one regret was that the bank returned to a policy of unconditional redemption in gold. They were not incorrect in considering the bank's retreat a result of my influence.

Naturally I was fully aware that public opinion in Austria was in favor of inflationism, and that aside from me there were few who supported a policy of stable exchange rates. The minister of finance at the time, Count Zaleski, was a Pole who had received his appointment on purely political grounds. He freely admitted to never before having dealt with financial problems. "Members of the Polish Club told me that a rise in foreign exchange rates must be seen as a favorable rather than unfavorable phenomenon," Zaleski explained to me in a conversation that took place in the home of a mutual friend. "For agriculture," he went on, "a ten-percent rise would be a direct blessing."

This blessing would soon come in good measure.

6

The Theory of Money and Credit

After completing the two essays on the bank's foreign-exchange policy, I intended to proceed with work on my theory of money and credit. I had barely written the first pages when, in early January 1909, I was called to special military duty. The so-called "annexation crisis" had caused the government to take extraordinary measures and speed up the modernization of the artillery. I returned to Vienna in February, and on April 1, entered the Viennese *Handelskammer*. I found no time for scientific work during the first months on the new job; it was not until the fall that I was able to begin. The finished manuscript was in the hands of the publisher early in 1912.

The greatest difficulty I faced in preparing the book was that I had intended to deal with only a portion of the broad scope of economic problems. But economics must necessarily be a closed, unified system. One cannot extract bits and pieces and study them independently. In economics, there is no such thing as specialization. Whoever deals with a part must do so on the basis of a theory that encompasses all problems. Gratitude is due the old masters, but I was finding that I could not use any of the existing theories. I was advancing further down the path they had discovered. The system of Menger and Böhm-Bawerk was no longer fully satisfying to me. In fact, I was displeased by their treatment of the problems with which monetary theory must begin.

The reigning notion at the time stated that the theory of money could be neatly separated from the broader structure of economic problems—that it did not, in fact, actually belong within the field of economics, and was to a certain extent a discipline unto itself. In accordance with this notion, universities in Anglo-Saxon countries created special professorships for currency and banking. But the notion was false; it was my intention to reveal its untenability and return the theory of money to the study of economics.

I had already begun writing my theory of direct exchange, and would have included it in the first volume along with the theory of indirect exchange had I been able to take my time and work in peace. But I knew that we were standing on the eve of a great war, and there was not much time available to me. I wanted to complete my book before the war's outbreak. Thus I made the decision to go beyond the narrow structure of monetary theory by a few points only, postponing a more comprehensive work. I believe the task was done justice.

I want to emphasize expressly that any quarrels I had with the works of Menger and Böhm-Bawerk had rather more to do with what they did not say than with what they did. I regretted their not having replaced John Stuart Mill's inadequate delineation of the field of economics with a more satisfactory one. I disapproved of their lack of sharp criticism concerning the even more inadequate use of mathematical economics, as well as their failure to elaborate more clearly on their own point of view. Above all, I found that Böhm, in his discussion with Wieser, had neglected to touch upon topics that were of decisive importance.

The problems of assumed measurement of value, and the related problem of total value were points within the theory of money that I could not silently ignore, despite their belonging to general value theory. That there existed such a thing as "value calculation" or even "value measurement—that "value" of a total supply could be calculated from the known "value" of a part, and, inversely, that the "value" of a part could be obtained from the "value" of a whole—were notions that needed to be refuted if a theory of money was to be developed. One had to actually eliminate hypostasis of "value," and demonstrate that there is an activity of valuing and there are acts of valuation, but that the term "value" is permissible only when limited to denoting an individually valued object, or to designating the result of a valuation process.

I disposed of these problems in the first few sections of my book, and in so doing, refuted the fallacies of Schumpeter and Irving Fischer. Cuhel's book[1] proved useful to me in all of this. The author is forgotten today and his book is outdated; but I do not doubt that he, in the end, will hold the place of honor due to him in the history of our science.

The theories on determination and changes of the purchasing power of money take Menger's theory of cash holding as a starting point. All further theories I had to construct anew. It is not my intention to present an excerpt from my book within these pages. I wish merely to remark on my method and its relevance.

Throughout my book I use the "step-by-step" method, a method being rediscovered today under the designations *period analysis* or *process analysis.* It is the only acceptable method. It renders the argument between *short-run* and *long-run economics* superfluous, and even the distinction between statics and dynamics becomes dispensable. If no condition is considered "normal"—if one is aware that the idea of "static equilibrium" has nothing to do with the life and action we study and is merely a mental image that is used in order to conceptualize human

[1] *Zur Lehre von den Bedürfnisse* (On the Theory of Needs).

action through a state of nonaction—then one must recognize that it is always motion we are studying, but never a state of equilibrium. All of mathematical economics, with its beautiful curves and equations, is idle flirtation. The setting up of equations and the drawing of curves must be preceded by nonmathematical considerations; the setting up of equations does not broaden our understanding. Mechanical equations can be used to solve practical problems through the introduction of empirically acquired constants and data; but equations of mathematical catallactics cannot in the same way be of service to practical problems in the area of human action where constant relations do not exist.

In my book on money I made no use of polemics directed against the mathematical school. I presented the correct doctrine and refrained from attacking the method of mathematicians. I even withstood the temptation to unravel the vacuous term "velocity." The death knell for mathematical economics was sounded when I proved that the money supply and spending power of the monetary unit are not inversely proportional. The proof demonstrated that the only constant relationship that was believed to have been found between "economic quantities" is in fact a variable determined by the data in each individual case. It also rendered Irving Fisher and Gustav Cassel's equations of exchange obsolete.

The step-by-step analysis must take into account the passage of time. The time lag between cause and effect becomes a multiplicity of time differences between single, successive consequences. Upon examining these lags in time, one is led to a precise theory of the social consequences of change in the purchasing power of money.

In order to shed some light on the objections I raised earlier concerning the teachings of Menger and Böhm-Bawerk and to give some concrete examples that illustrate the difference between the older and the younger Austrian schools, I must address Böhm-Bawerk's reaction to my theory. Both Menger and Böhm-Bawerk tacitly assumed the neutrality of money. They had developed the theory of direct exchange and held to the opinion that all problems of economic theory could be solved without the imaginary notion of money-free market exchanges. This teaching was now made untenable by my theory of the inevitable non-neutrality of money. But Böhm refused to admit this. He raised no objections to the cogency of my step-by-step analysis; he did not deny its results—namely, that changes in purchasing power of money cause prices of different commodities and services to change neither simultaneously nor evenly, and that it is incorrect to maintain that changes in the quantity of money, yield simultaneous and proportional changes in the "level" of prices. But he did maintain that this was a "friction phenomenon." The old doctrine was correct "in principle," according to Böhm. It would retain its full significance for an analysis of "purely economic action." Reality presents resistance and friction, however, which would cause the result to deviate from that which would have been arrived at theoretically. I tried in vain to convince Böhm of the inadmissibility of the use of metaphors borrowed from mechanics. One can see in his twofold arrangement of the tasks of the price theory that Böhm was heavily influenced by the ideas of John Stuart Mill.[2] I could have convinced him had only I been clear about the basic problems. But I myself was still operating under the influence of Mill. It was only years later that I would be able to refute Böhm-Bawerk's doctrine of "direct exchange advantage."[3] Writing the essay devoted to a critique of the doctrines of Menger and Böhm, I believe, was a way of erecting a lasting memorial to the two masters.

---

[2]Böhm-Bawerk, *Kapital und Kapitalismus* (Capital and Interest).

[3]"Grundprobleme der Nationalökonomie."

In the chapter dealing with the structuring of exchange ratios between different kinds of money I sought to restate Ricardo's irrefutable doctrine, which had been suppressed by the "balance of payment" theory. Soon thereafter, Gustav Cassel presented Ricardo's doctrine in inexpedient form and designated it the "purchasing power parity theory." During the 1920s it was called one of two things: Cassel's theory, if one agreed with it, and Mises's theory, if one rejected it. But I repeat: it is Ricardo's theory.

The second large problem with which my book dealt was that of fiduciary media. I had to create this new term in order to overcome the prevailing confusion surrounding the use of the term "credit." If no distinction is made between the terms "commodity credit"[4] and "fiduciary credit,"[5] (Machlup offers the clever translations *transfer credit* and *created credit*), useful results can never be achieved. It is only by first making this distinction that the foundation can be laid for a correct critique of the doctrine of "elasticity" of bank media of payment; with this distinction the way is made free for the monetary theory of business cycle phenomena. I was given the honor of naming it the Austrian Trade Cycle Theory.

In the last section of my book, my concern was to discuss items that were of general interest at the time, namely, currency and banking problems. In concluding my book, I pointed out that prevailing notions on banking would soon lead to catastrophic events.

As could be expected, my book was rejected by German scientific journals in a most precipitous manner. I paid this little attention. I knew that my views would soon take hold. I saw with horror the catastrophe which I had predicted standing before the door.

---

[4] *Sachkredit.*

[5] *Zirkulationskredit.*

New books that are "destroyed" by critics are lasting and valuable. He who only says what others want to hear is better off remaining silent. Knapp, Benedix, Liefmann, Diehl, Adolf Wagner, and Bortkiewicz, all celebrated "monetary theorists" in Germany at the time, have been forgotten.

The first economist to give my work any credit was B.M. Anderson in his book, *The Value of Money*, which appeared in 1919. Because Austria was at war with the United States, it was two years later that I first caught a glimpse of it.

John Maynard Keynes reviewed my book in the first issue of the *Economics Journal* that appeared after the outbreak of the war.[6] Mr. Keynes gave the book some praise: "the book is not to be denied considerable merits . . . the book is enlightened in the highest degree possible." But on the whole, Mr. Keynes was greatly disappointed.

My book seemed to him "not constructive" and "not original;" there is "no lift in the book." And he added, "One closes the book, therefore, with a feeling of disappointment that an author so intelligent, so candid and so widely read should, after all, help one so little to a clear understanding of the fundamentals of his subject." Sixteen years later,[7] Keynes admitted that his knowledge of the German language was lacking. "In German," he said, "I can only understand what I know already—so that new ideas are apt to be veiled from me by the difficulties of the language." It was not my fault that Keynes found my book neither original nor constructive, and that it could not bring him to a clear understanding of the problems.

---

[6]*Economic Journal* XXIV(1914): 417–19.

[7]Keynes, *A Treatise on Money*, London 1930, Bd. I, S.199, Anmerkung 2.

7

The First World War

I need not report on the war or on my personal experiences during the war in this work; I concern myself with military questions and with the political only to the extent that they aid in making my aim more accessible.

The war came as a result of an ideology that had been proclaimed from German lecterns for hundreds of years. Professors of economics had contributed to the intellectual preparation for war. They did not first need to be retrained in order to become "intellectual bodyguards of the Hohenzollern." Schmoller authored the famous "Manifesto of 93" (October 11, 1914), another professor, Schumacher, who succeeded Schmoller in Berlin, edited the annexation program of the six central associations. Sombart wrote *Händler und Helden*.[1] Franz Oppenheimer could not do enough to attack the lack of culture in England and France. Economics was no longer taught; what was taught were the doctrines of war.

---

[1]"Merchants and Heroes"; sometimes translated as "Hucksters and Heroes."

Things were not much better in enemy camps, but there one could find many who preferred silence. Edwin Cannan considered it the duty of the economist to protest.

I was hardly able to read the newspaper during the first fifteen months of the war. Conditions improved a little later on. By the end of 1917, I was no longer at the front, but worked in Vienna in the economics division of the Department of War. I wrote only two small essays during those years. The one concerning the classification of monetary theories was later added to the second edition of *The Theory of Money and Credit*. The other, *The Objectives of Foreign Trade Policy*,[2] I made use of when writing *Nation, State, and Economy*,[3] published in 1919. It was a scientific book, but its intent was political. It was an attempt to alienate public opinion in Germany and Austria from yet unnamed national-socialist ideals, as well as promote reconstruction through democratic-liberal policy. Little attention was paid to my work; the book was seldom read. But I know that it will be read in time. The few friends who are reading it today do not doubt this.

Toward the end of the war I published a short essay on quantity theory in the journal of the Association of Austrian Banks and Bankers, a journal intended for its members but not for public consumption. My calm, academic treatment of the problem of inflation was rejected by the censor, and I had to revise it before it could appear. Responses were run in the very next issue. One of these, if I remember correctly, came from bank director Rosenbaum, who was financing Federn's *Economist*.

In the summer of 1918 the Army Supreme Command organized a course for officers who were to offer patriotic

---

[2]"Vom Ziel der Handelspolitik."

[3]*Nation, Staat und Wirtschaft*.

instructions to the troops. In my presentation, "War Costs and War Loans," I attempted to oppose the inflationary tendencies. My lecture was published from stenographic notes, and I was never given the opportunity to read the proofs.

My experiences during wartime turned my attention toward a problem that has become more important to me day by day; indeed, I want to call it the principle and fundamental problem of our culture.

He alone who fully understands economic theory can comprehend the great questions of economic and social policy. He alone who masters the most difficult tasks of economics can determine where capitalism, socialism, or interventionism constitute suitable systems of social cooperation. Political decisions, however, are not made by economists, but by public opinion, that is, the general public. The majority determines what should happen. This is true of all systems of government. Even absolute kings and dictators must govern in accordance with the demands of public opinion.

There are schools of thought that simply do not want to recognize these problems. The contention of orthodox Marxism is that the dialectical process of historical development unconsciously guides man on the essential path; that is, the path that leads to his salvation. Another variety of Marxism is of the persuasion that the class can never err. Race mysticism maintains the same concerning race: the characteristics of the race intuit the finding of right solutions. Religious mysticism, even where it appears in worldly garb, for example, the führer principle, relies on God: He will never forsake His children, but protect them from evil through revelation or by sending them a blessed Shepherd. But experience spares us these escapes. It shows us that there are different doctrines and different opinions, even within various classes, races, and nations; it shows us that different men vie for leadership with different agendas, and that different churches come forth to proclaim the Word of God. One would have to be blind to claim that the question of whether interest rates can be permanently reduced by credit expansion could be answered by an appeal to the dialectics of history, an unerring class consciousness, racial or national characteristics, God's Word, or a führer's order.

Liberals of the eighteenth century were filled with a boundless optimism that said, Mankind is rational, and therefore right ideas will triumph in the end. Light will replace darkness; the efforts of bigots to keep people in a state of ignorance in order to rule them more easily cannot prevent progress. Enlightened by reason, mankind is moving toward ever-greater perfection. Democracy, with its freedom of thought, speech, and of the press guarantees the success of the right doctrine: let the masses decide; they will make the most appropriate choice.

We no longer share this optimism. The conflict of economic doctrines makes far greater demands on our ability to make judgments than did the conflicts encountered during the period of enlightenment: superstition and natural science, tyranny and freedom, privilege and equality before the law.

The people must decide. It is indeed the duty of economists to inform their fellow citizens. But what should happen if economists do not measure up to the dialectic task and become pushed aside by demagogues, or if the people lack the intelligence to grasp their teachings? With the awareness that men like J.M. Keynes, Bertrand Russell, Harold Laski, and Albert Einstein could not comprehend the problems of economics, must not the attempt to guide the masses in the proper direction be considered hopeless?

One is mistaken and fails to understand what is involved if one expects help to come in the form of a new election system or from some improvement in public education. Proposed changes to the election system would result in a portion of the masses' being denied the right to vote for legislators and other administrators. This offers no solution, for when an administration put into place by a minority has no popular support it is not sustainable over the long term. If it refuses to yield to public opinion, it will be overthrown by revolution. The advantage of the democratic system consists in the fact that it makes possible a peaceable alignment of the government system and its personnel with the will of the people. This, in turn, guarantees the continuance of uninterrupted and untroubled social cooperation within the state. Concerns taken up here are not just those having to do with democracy. Indeed, they are much more than that: they are concerns that exist under all circumstances and under every conceivable form of government.

It has been said that the problem lay within the realms of public education and public information. But we are badly deceived if we believe that the right opinions will claim victory through the circulation of books and journals and with more schools and lectures; such means can also attract followers of faulty doctrines. Evil consists precisely in the fact that the masses are not intellectually enabled to choose the means leading to their desired objectives. That ready judgments can be foisted onto the people through the power of suggestion demonstrates that the people are not capable of making independent decisions. Herein lies the great danger.

Thus had I arrived at the hopeless pessimism that had long pervaded the best minds of Europe. We know today from the letters of Jacob Burckhardt that this great historian, too, harbored no illusions about the future of European civilization. This pessimism had broken the will of Carl Menger. It had cast a shadow over the life of Max Weber, who had become a good friend of mine while spending a semester at the University of Vienna during the last months of war.

How one carries on in the face of unavoidable catastrophe is a matter of temperament. In high school, as was custom, I had chosen a verse by Virgil to be my motto: *Tu ne cede malis sed contra audentior ito* ("Do not give in to evil, but proceed ever more boldly against it"). I recalled these words during the darkest hours of the war. Again and again I had met with situations from which rational deliberation found no means of escape; but then the unexpected intervened, and with it came salvation. I would not lose courage even now. I wanted to do everything an economist could do. I would not tire in saying what I knew to be true. I thus decided to write a book about socialism. I had considered the plan before the beginning of the war; now I wanted to carry it out.

8

With the *Handelskammer*[1]

Before I proceed with a description of my scientific endeavors, I must address my practical activity. From 1909 to 1938 I served with the "Niederösterreichischen Handels- und Gewerbe Kammer."[2] (In 1920 the name of this institution was changed to the "Wiener Kammer für Handel, Gewerbe, und Industrie."[3])

In Austria the *Handelskammer* was a parliamentary body composed of elected businessmen. These were financed through a surtax on the occupational tax that was collected by the internal revenue service and then transferred to them. It had been formed during the revolution in 1848 in order to advise the government and Parliament on economic matters, and to take up some administrative duties. Until the latter part of the 1870s it

---

[1]Chamber of Commerce.

[2]Lower Austrian Chamber of Commerce and Industry.

[3]Vienna Chamber of Commerce, Handicrafts, and Industry.

remained rather insignificant. In the 1880s and 1890s it led a futile campaign against the sectarian reforms promoted and pushed through by the Christian Social Party. Throughout this time the bulk of *Handelskammer* activity lay within the general assembly and in *Handelskammer* committees. The *Handelskammer*'s office merely did busy work.

The breakthrough of interventionism brought with it a radical change. Secretaries, department officials, and Parliament members were completely ignorant when it came to matters of economics. They had, for the most part, no awareness of the consequences of the measures they took, and were barely capable of shaping laws, decrees, and regulations in a way that allowed officers charged with carrying them out to understand what needed to be done. It became imperative to seek appropriate advice and continued cooperation with persons who knew the conditions or were in the position to give instruction. The Parliament, the press, and the Kaiser took the secretaries to task for mistakes that were made on a daily basis, which the secretaries in turn saw as the responsibility of the departmental officials. In order to escape this responsibility, they sought the advice of men knowledgeable in their field.

Rudolf Maresch and Richard Riedl, secretaries of the Viennese *Handelskammer*, knew to use these favorable conditions to expand the influence of their office. The president of the *Handelskammer* at the time was the long-sighted Baron Mauthner. He played a prominent role in the House of Representatives as the leader of the Mauthner group, which had been named for him. (The *Handelskammer* sent special delegates to the House of Representatives until 1907, and to the Parliament until 1918.) Mauthner agreed to the expansion of the secretary's office, and several young economists were added to the staff. The most distinguished among them was my friend Viktor Graetz, a man of unusual gifts and sturdy character who, precisely because of his clear vision, suffered from the same pessimism that was destined to befall all men of insight during this time. The success of this new course in the *Handelskammer* was tremendous. In a short time the secretary's office became an important factor in determining economic policy. Its importance grew even further when it, under the designation *Handelspolitische Zentralstelle*,[4] created an organization in which all Austrian *Handelskammers* played a part. Surely enough, many a provincial *Handelskammer* was irrelevant because its secretary exercised no influence. But secretaries from Prague, Brno, Reichenberg, Krakow, and Trieste were men whose participation was exceedingly valuable.

In 1909, the continuation of the Vienna *Handelskammer*'s management came into question. Maresch had been retired for a number of years, and 1909 brought Riedl's appointment as head of the trade division of the Department of Commerce. Several young officers had left the *Handelskammer* to work in industry, and my friend, Graetz, left in order to assume the management of a larger enterprise. He recommended me as his successor.

The *Handelskammer* offered me the only arena in which I could work in Austria. A university professorship was closed to me; sought after were interventionists and socialists. Anyone not belonging to one of the three parties (the Christian Socialist, the German National, and the Social Democratic Parties) could not hope for an appointment. Nor did I aspire to a position in government service. After the war my expertise in money and banking was so widely recognized that many of the banks offered me a position on their boards. But until 1921 I always declined, as I was not given the assurance that my advice would be followed. Later I considered banks insolvent and irretrievably lost; events proved me right.

I created my position myself. Officially, I was no more than an employee in the office of the secretary. Nominally, I was always under a superior and had colleagues. I never had the

---

[4]The Center for Trade Policy.

desire to manage the agency or to dedicate my productive powers to bureaucratic routines. My position was incomparable to, and of greater importance than, that of any other *Handelskammer* official or any other Austrian not heading up of one of the large political parties. I was the economist of the land.

This is not to say that my recommendations were carried out, or that what I discouraged remained undone. Supported by few friends, I waged a hopeless battle. A postponement of the catastrophe was all I accomplished. That events did not result in Bolshevism in the winter of 1918/1919 and that the collapse of banks and industry occurred in 1931 instead of 1921 were largely due to the success of my efforts. More could not be achieved, at least not by me.

To be sure, not everything that happened in the *Handelskammer* met with my approval. I did not concern myself with the purely administrative goings on. I concentrated all of my energies on crucial economic and political questions.

I was sometimes accused of representing my viewpoint in a manner too abrupt and intransigent. It was also claimed that I could have accomplished more had I displayed a greater willingness to compromise. Gustav Weiss von Wellenstein, an old friend and the secretary general of the Central Association for Austrian Industry often lectured me on the same. The criticism was unwarranted; I could only be effective if I could present things as they appeared to me. When I look back at my work with the *Handelskammer* today, my only regret is my willingness to compromise, and not my intransigence. I was always prepared to give in on the minor issues if it meant that those more important could be salvaged. Occasionally I made intellectual sacrifices by signing reports that included statements that did not reflect my view. This was the only possible way to ensure a report's gaining public approval or acceptance by the general assembly of the *Handelskammer*.

Were one to search the *Handelskammer*'s published progress and business reports, or even its archives, one would find confirmation of this claim. I have never viewed the reports and petitions that name me as reporting officer as my work, but as an expression of the opinion of that institution which I served as a consultant. I have always drawn a sharp line between my scientific and my political activity. In science, compromise is a betrayal of truth. But compromise is essential in politics, where results can oftentimes only be achieved through the reconciliation of conflicting views. Science is an accomplishment of the individual, and not, by definition, a collaborative effort. Politics is always a collaboration of men and often means compromise.

I was the economic conscience of postwar Austria. I was helped by few, and distrusted by all political parties. And yet all secretaries and party leaders sought my advice and wanted to hear my opinion. I never attempted to force my views upon them, nor did I ever seek out a statesman or politician. On no occasion did I appear in the lobby of Parliament or a government department without having first received a formal invitation. Secretaries and party leaders visited my office more often than I visited theirs.

I enjoyed working with my colleagues in the *Handelskammer*. Many of them were men of great knowledge and ability who strongly supported my efforts.

My job with the *Handelskammer* greatly expanded my horizons. That I now have the material for a social and economic history of the downfall of the Austrian civilization readily at hand is to a large degree the result of the studying that was required for me to be able to carry on with my work in the *Handelskammer*. Travels that led me to all parts of old Austria-Hungary from 1912–1914 taught me much in particular. In visiting the centers of industry, my intent was to become acquainted with the industrial situation in view of the renewal of customs and trade relations with Hungary, and the adoption of new, autonomous tariffs and trade treaties.

The main thrust of my job with the *Handelskammer* was not dealing with commercial questions, but those pertaining to finance, currency, credit, and tax policy. In addition, I was given special assignments on an ongoing basis. From the time of the armistice until the signing of the Peace Agreement of Saint Germain I was the consultant on financial questions to the Foreign Office. Later, when the terms of the peace treaty were put into effect, I was in charge of the office concerned with prewar debt. In this capacity I had numerous dealings with the representatives of our former enemies. I was the Austrian delegate to the international *Handelskammer* and a member of many international commissions and committees, whose insoluble task it was to facilitate the peaceful exchange of goods and services in a world pervaded by national hatred and the precursors of genocide.

In 1926 I founded the Austrian Institute for Business Cycle Research. Along with Dollfuss[5] and Edmund Palla, the secretary of the Chamber of Labor, I belonged to the three-member publication committee of the Economic Commission, which, with the cooperation of Professor Richard Schüller, published a report on Austria's economic difficulties.

It is not necessary for the purpose of this manuscript to say more about the multifaceted jobs that consumed my time while with the *Handelskammer*. It was hard work, and the many trivialities were often quite burdensome. But this is uninteresting, and I prefer to address the political aims that gave my work direction.

My political activity from 1918 to 1934 can be broken down into four stages.

The most important task I undertook during the first period, which lasted from the time of the monarchy's collapse in the fall of 1918 until the fall of 1919, was the forestalling of a Bolshevist takeover. The fact that events did not lead to such a regime in

---

[5]Engelbert Dolfuss, rising leader of the Christian Socialist Party and later Austrian Chancellor.

Vienna was my success and mine alone. Few supported me in my efforts, and any help was relatively ineffective. I have already mentioned the success of my influence with Otto Bauer in this regard. I alone convinced Bauer to abandon the idea of seeking union with Moscow. Bauer's authority was not acknowledged by the radical young, who wanted to forge ahead on their own and against the will of party leadership. But they were so inexperienced, incapable, and torn by internal rivalries that they were unable to found a halfway viable communist party organization. Forward motion lay in the hands of the leaders of the old Social Democratic Party, in whose circle Bauer had the final word.

When this danger had been overcome, I directed all of my efforts toward putting an end to inflation. In this battle I had found an outstanding comrade in Wilhelm Rosenberg, a student of Carl Menger who had remained true to his friendship with his old teacher. He was a sharp thinker, an excellent economist, and such a brilliant lawyer that his advice was sought on all difficult questions of a business or financial nature. He enjoyed the high esteem afforded an "expert" on financial matters, and was prepared to use this privilege as he took on the fight against inflation.

We fought for three years before we achieved our goal: the restoration of a balanced budget and the cessation of a further increase in banknotes. It was to our credit alone that the Austrian crown was stabilized at a ratio of 14,400 paper crowns to one gold crown, and not at a higher rate. But this was not the result we had sought.

Had it not been for our passionate agitation against the continuation of the deficit and inflation policy, it is highly likely that the crown would have fallen to one millionth or one billionth of its 1892 gold parity in early 1922. It is unlikely that any administration would have then been able to maintain public order. Foreign troops would have had to occupy the country, and foreign powers would have created a new state. This catastrophe was avoided. An Austrian administration had eliminated the deficit and stabilized the crown. Austria's currency did not collapse, as did Germany's in 1923. The crack up boom did not occur. Nevertheless, the country had to bear the destructive consequences of continuing inflation for many years. Its banking, credit, and insurance systems had suffered wounds that could no longer heal, and no halt could be put to the consumption of capital. We met with too much resistance. Our victory had come too late. It had postponed the collapse by many years, but it could no longer save Austria.

Rosenberg and I suffered no illusions on this matter. We knew the truth surrounding the restoration. My friend succumbed to the pessimism borne of hopelessness, the lot of all enlightened Austrians. It was not only the grief of having lost his only son, but the knowledge of the futility of his toils in Vienna that drove him to his death.

Our success in the struggle for a balanced budget was delayed because it took us so long to convince the Christian Socialist Party of the necessity of eliminating state subsidies intended to reduce the retail price on rationed foodstuffs. This reduction played only a minor role in the consumer budget, but it precluded the restoration of a balance in the government's budget. Thanks to the support of Weiss-Wellenstein[6], we were successful in persuading large industry to grant concessions to labor unions were the subsidies to cease. The fact that the labor unions agreed to our plan behind their backs was a heavy blow to Social Democrat Party leaders. Otto Bauer took desperate measures to disrupt the negotiations. On December 1, 1921, the *Ordner*,[7] Social Democratic Party troops, stormed the inner city and plundered and demolished all retail stores. The police, opting to retain political neutrality, did nothing to interfere. In the days that followed, however, the public voiced its opposition to

---

[6]Gustav Weiss-Wellenstein, Austrian industrialist.

[7]The Organizers.

such tactics, the Social Democrats retreated, and negotiations with labor unions were resumed.

One must not underestimate the credit that is due Christian Social Party leader, Professor Seipel.[8] He was a stranger to economics in a sense that only a cleric could be. He saw inflation as an evil, but was otherwise inexperienced when it came to financial policy. Rosenberg and I felt obliged to bring to his attention the fact that a stabilization of the currency would in time allow the consequences of inflation to become outcropped in the form of a "stabilization crisis." We explained to him that public opinion would place responsibility for the depression that would follow the inflation boom on the combatants of inflation, and not on those who caused it. The Christian Social Party would harvest ingratitude rather than thanks.

Seipel appreciated our candor. He felt that useful and necessary measures must be taken, even if they meant damage to the party. The statesman distinguishes himself from the demagogue in that he prefers that which is right over that which brings him acclaim. There were not many politicians in Austria who shared this kind of thinking. Although his worldview and life notions remained foreign to me, I felt the highest respect for the genteel and honest character of this noble priest. He was a noteworthy personality.

His lack of worldliness, unfortunately, had damaging effects on his politics. The corruption of his colleagues, Christian Social and German National Party members, was not plain to him. He failed to notice that his party friends thought only of personal gain.

These party friends, in particular Deputy Viktor Keinboeck, an attorney who later became minister of finance and then president

---

[8]Seipel served as Chancellor during the 1920s and was an ordained Catholic priest. He held a Ph.D. in political science.

of the National Bank, had introduced him to Gottfried Kunwald, the son of an eminent Viennese attorney. Kunwald had been disabled since birth. He labored to take but few steps, hobbling from one room to the next. He required constant care and attention, and was always accompanied by two strong men who lifted him out of the car or helped him up and down the stairs. Bravely overcoming all of these constraints, Kunwald had finished his studies and earned his doctorate in law. The bar was inaccessible to him, as his physical condition did not allow for him to complete the requisite, yearlong internship. But he found an occupation in the law office founded by his father and carried forth by his brother-in-law. Being an outstanding and knowledgeable jurist, he had a large clientele.

Kunwald was well read but could not think in economic terms. He saw economic problems with the eyes of a jurist who prepared contracts. But he was opposed to inflation, having seen the disruption it caused in the economy, and was thus prepared to support Rosenberg and me as we initiated the fight against it.

Kunwald enjoyed the boundless confidence of a number of Christian Social politicians and a few bankers whom he advised on difficult legal matters. The dealings of these friends of Kunwald were not always without objection. These politicians capitalized ruthlessly on their positions in public life, receiving compensation for commissions of all kinds, supporting bids for public contracts, and exerting influence over many agencies. They had profited greatly during times of inflation, and feared that stabilization would jeopardize their interests. Kunwald explained to them that the inflation would soon meet its end in any case, and hinted that he would find remunerative opportunities for them in its wake.

When Rosenberg and I succeeded in winning Seipel and his party over to monetary stabilization, they chose Kunwald as their liaison officer and charged him with implementation of the necessary measures. He proved himself at first equal and true to the task, and our work together went well, overall. He had gathered around himself a circle of bankers, government officials, and Christian Social politicians with whom he conducted a kind of financial political seminar. But as years passed and his activity continued, his influence became menacing. The outstanding purpose of his instruction became the confutation or weakening of my critique of the prevailing interventionist policy. In his view, it was not as bad as I had presented it; Austria was making economic progress, and there should be no talk of interventionist policy leading only to capital consumption.

I know for certain that Kunwald was not acting in good faith in his optimistic presentation. He had in fact rightly judged the situation of the banks and large enterprises and had occasionally made comments that were no less pessimistic than mine. But he believed that his influence with the secretaries, through whom he secured license and other favors for his clients, would suffer were he to present the plain truth about the state of affairs. He relied on this influence for his income as an attorney and financial agent.

It was extraordinarily difficult to counteract Kunwald's unfavorable influence. One could not freely discuss such matters in public if the credit reputation of the Austrian economy were to be protected. It would have been easy to present the facts in such a way that everyone appreciated the necessity of abandoning the policy of capital consumption. But in so doing, the bank's foreign credits would have been undermined, and bankruptcy would have been unavoidable. I was forced, therefore, to use extraordinary restraint in my efforts to bring about a change in economic policies lest I alarm the public and unsettle the credit of banks and industry. This restraint guided my conduct throughout the third period, beginning with the stabilization of the crown in 1922 and lasting until the collapse of the *Kreditanstalt* in the spring of 1931.[9] The worse the situation became,

---

[9]The *Kreditanstalt* was Austria's largest banking institution, closely tied to the Austrian branch of the house of Rothschild. It collapsed on May 14, 1931, after which it was taken over by the Austrian government.

due to the continuation of calamitous policies, the greater the danger of a credit crisis and the more important it became not to disturb foreign markets. After the collapse of the *Bodenkreditanstalt* in 1929,[10] I myself insisted that a graphic presentation of Austrian industrial progress after 1922 be made at a London exhibition. It was clear to me as well as to Hayek, who as head of the Institute for Business Cycle Research had prepared the tables, that this progress was questionable. Having used only statistically unobjectionable data, however, I saw no harm in making known abroad what appeared as progress within the prevailing mercantilist point of view.

Taking into consideration the precarious credit situation, I never offered a whitewashed rendition of the conditions, nor did I tolerate suppression, much less falsification of statistical data. I had the institute prepare an investigation into capital consumption for the previously mentioned commission. The bank had objections when the publication committee made plans to reveal the results of this investigation in its report. At the time I already knew of the approaching banking crisis, and wanted to avoid everything that might hasten its outbreak. The concerns of the bank were unfounded, and I agreed that the publication of the inquiry should be carried out, not under the name of the economic commission or of the institute, but under that of the head of the institute, Oskar Morgenstern.

My work during this third period of my political activity in postwar Austria was even more tedious than that of the two earlier periods. The tedium stemmed from daily battles against ignorance, inability, indolence, malice, and corruption. I did not stand alone in the fight. Dear, good friends assisted me, in

---

[10]The *Bodenkreditanstalt* was a real estate lender that had itself swallowed several other unhealthy banks. After its collapse in 1929, Vienna authorities asked the *Kreditanstalt* to absorb the failed lender.

particular Siegfried Strakosch von Feldringen, Gustav Weiss von Wellenstein, and Victor Graetz. The support I received from my assistant in the *Handelskammer*, Therese Wolf-Thieberger, was of special value. Her extraordinary intelligence, her indefatigability in work, and her personal bravery helped me through the dark hours.

The use of the catchword *Lebensunfähigkeit*[11] with regard to Austria had had a damaging effect through the years. Everyone in Austria and abroad was convinced that Austria was not "viable." It was believed that a "small" country could not retain its independence, especially when it needed to import essential raw materials. For this reason it was thought that Austria should seek merger with some larger economic entity, that is, with the German Reich.

Outside of Austria, even those circles that had inserted the annexation prohibition into the Peace Treaty of Saint Germain held to this view. They recommended special economic privileges in order to make possible a continuation of Austria's political independence. In this spirit, the *Völkerbundanliehe*, or League of Nations loan, was granted to assist in Seipel's crown stabilization in 1922. Austria did not need a foreign loan at this time; what it did need was a foreign finance commissioner whom the government could, if necessary, hold responsible for the odium: the vetoing of an increase in outlays. The League of Nations appointed a finance commissioner by the name of Alfred Zimmerman, an ignorant, tactless, and arrogant Dutchman. Hans Patzauer, an official in the Ministry of Finance, conducted business in Zimmerman's name. Patzauer was a highly gifted man, knowledgeable, firm in character, and equal to the tasks presented him. He died shortly before the end of Zimmerman's term and before having reached the age of fifty. Precisely how necessary this financial guardianship was to the Austrian

[11]Literally, "inviability" or lack of capacity for survival.

state would become evident when, just a few hours after its termination, the government guaranteed the obligations of the insolvent *Zentralbank deutscher Sparkassen*.[12]

Besides the granting of this League of Nations loan and another in 1932, the western powers did nothing to assist Austria. After the Nazis raised obstacles preventing the export of Austrian lumber to Germany, the French government was petitioned, in vain, to grant tariff reductions on lumber exports to France.

German Nationalists, who had called themselves the party for a "Greater Germany" since the collapse of the monarchy, saw in the myth of Austria's *Lebensunfähigkeit* a sweeping argument for annexation. For the Christian Socialists, who feigned support of the annexation while actually doing everything they could to prevent it, this myth served as a convenient means to sabotage all attempts to steer economic policy in a reasonable direction. After all, they said, ours is not a viable existence, and it is therefore pointless to seek life-giving economic policies. It would have appeared downright unpatriotic to suggest reforms that could improve the economic situation. The theory of the *Lebensunfähigkeit* of Austria was considered the most important of foreign policy's assets; with its help, one would be able to demand favors of all kinds from the western powers. Anyone contradicting this thinking, as did Friedrich Otto Hertz, was seen as a traitor.

It is not necessary to expound on just how untenable the theory of *Lebensunfähigkeit* of small countries is. But I do want to point out just how contradictory the appeal to the alleged doctrine was in the mouths of the protectionists who had come into power. Industry in postwar Austria suffered less from the dissolution of the old monarchy's tariff zone than did its counterpart in the Sudetenland. Since 1918, when they were freed from the pressures of Sudetenland competition, several Austrian industries had been able to expand their production. Other industries, for

[12]The central reserve bank of the German savings banks.

example the sugar industry, had only recently come into existence in Austria. In the old tariff zone, Austria's agriculture industry was in a difficult position when compared to that of Hungary. But now, thanks to a prohibitive trade policy, Austria could greatly expand its production.

The fact that coal had to be imported was no disadvantage, considering the unfavorable conditions in the coal market. It must be noted in general that during the Great Depression that began in 1929, prices of raw materials fell further and more rapidly than those of industrial products; industrial countries were not hit as hard as agricultural and raw-materials countries. Austria was not justified in joining in on the complaining about the fall in prices for raw materials.

Financially, too, the new Austria suffered less from the dissolution of the old state than did other parts of the empire. In the old empire the government had used some of the Austrian tax revenues to cover the administrative costs of its other members. The old Austria had not lived on the revenues of other members, for example, those of Galicia or Dalmatia, but had, on the contrary, subsidized them.

It has been said that Austria had to take on a disproportionate share of the administrative apparatus of the old empire. This, too, is incorrect. The new Austria inherited a small number of civil servants, mostly employees of the state-run railroad, who had been working in other divisions of the empire. The precise number could never be determined, as officials frustrated every attempt to do so. But there is no doubt that the number of civil servants in question was far less than one thousand. At the same time, and especially in the case of the railroads, there were many thousands, in fact tens of thousands, of individuals newly appointed. The surplus of civil servants in the new Austria had nothing to do with the legacy of the old empire.

The paralyzing effect of the catchword *Lebensunfähigkeit* cannot be assessed highly enough. Wherever a reform proposal appeared, it was rejected immediately on the basis of this catchword. The notorious term, *Schlamperei*[13] and the unfortunate, "*da laßt sich nix machen*,"[14] found in it a generally accepted justification.

The situation caused me to waver at times in my position on the annexation program. I was not blind to the dangers that would threaten Austrian culture if allied to the German Reich. But there were moments in which I asked myself whether the annexation was not a lesser evil than the continuation of a policy leading, unfailingly, toward catastrophe.

Since the currency reform in 1922, a coalition of the Christian Social Party and the Party for a Greater Germany had been the nominal rulers of Austria. The Social Democrats stood in opposition, holding "bourgeois" parties responsible for all deficiencies in the existing system. Surely enough, the situation was quite different in reality. The bulk of all executive power lay in the hands of individual state governments, elected by state legislatures. The power of the central state, that is, the federal parliament and the federal government, was limited. In the most important, richest and most populous state, the city of Vienna, the Social Democratic Party exercised absolute sovereignty, using its position of power to wage a ruthless war of destruction against the capitalist order. The second most important state, Lower Austria, was ruled by a coalition of Social Democrats and the Christian Social Party and there the Greater Germans comprised the opposition. In the state of Styria, the third in importance, the Social Democrats governed in likewise fashion. It was only in the smaller states, those less populous and financially successful, that the Social Democrats made up the opposition.

The effective predominance of the Social Democratic Party had nothing to do with parliamentary representation and its participation in government. It had to do with its terror apparatus.

---

[13]"Slovenliness."

[14]"There is nothing that can be done about the situation."

The party ruled all labor unions, in particular those of the railroad, the postal service, the telegraph and the telephone employees. The party could paralyze all economic life at any time through the imposition of a strike; it threatened strike in essential industries as soon as it disapproved of something in the government's position, thereby forcing the government to yield. What carried even more weight, however, was that the Social Democratic Party had at its disposal an army equipped with rifles and machine guns, light artillery, ample munitions, and manpower at least three times greater than that available to the government with its troops of federal forces and state and local police. Federal forces possessed neither tanks, nor heavy artillery, nor airplanes, all of which had been prohibited by the peace treaty. Disarmament provisions were strictly supervised by the military attachés of the western powers, who were more lenient with the Social Democrats. During the months following the armistice and the ratification of the peace treaty, Social Democrats had been permitted to secure from the stores of the old army as many weapons and as much ammunition as they wanted to and were able to take. They were later allowed the acquisition of weapons and ammunition from Czechoslovakia. The Social Democratic Army, officially called "The Organizers," conducted demonstrations and field exercises that the government was unable to oppose. Unchallenged, the Social Democrats assumed the "right to the street."

This right had already been extorted by the Social Democrats in the old empire. In the stir that in 1907 led to the adoption of universal, equal, and direct voting rights for the Austrian Parliament, the Social Democratic Party had tried to force the government and Parliament into compliance through terror and intimidation. The Austrian constitution had expressly prohibited open-air meetings at the time and in the vicinity of Parliament's sessions in order to assure that decisions could be made without regard to public opinion in the capital. In 1907, Vienna was already more heavily represented in Parliament than its number of inhabitants would have demanded. Nevertheless, the Social Democrats paid the prohibition no heed, and the imperial government shrank away. Work came to a complete standstill in Vienna on November 28, 1905, when 250,000 workers, in military rows of eight and under the leadership of party officials, marched down the *Ringstrasse*[15]and past Parliament. On that particular evening I happened upon Otto Bauer in a coffeehouse. He was much inebriated by the success of the demonstration. He was pleased to announce that the Social Democrats had now won the "right to the street," and would know how to preserve it for all future time. I was of another opinion. I asked him: "What will happen if another party at some point takes the street through organized force? Will this not lead to civil war?" Bauer's answer was quite characteristic:

> Such a question could only be asked by a bourgeois who does not realize that the future belongs to us alone. Where should such a party come from: a party that would dare to confront the organized proletariat? Once we have come to power, there will be no more resistance.

Marxism made the Social Democrats blind and stupid. During the early years of the Austrian Republic, I once heard the Social Democratic Mayor Seitz remark, "The rule of Social Democracy in Vienna is now secured forever. A child in kindergarten is already instilled with a proletarian consciousness. The schools teach Social Democracy, and labor unions complete this education. A Viennese is born into Social Democracy, lives in it, and dies as he has lived."

I incurred the disapproval of all present when I reduced my reply to a Viennese saying: "*Es sollen auch schon vierstöckige Hausherren gestorben sein*."[16]

---

[15]The main avenue encircling the old city of Vienna.

[16] Roughly translated, "Even the best laid plans can go awry."

As early as the winter of 1918/1919, the terror caused by the Social Democrats forced other Austrians to try to expand their defenses. After various failures, the "Home Guard" achieved some organizational success. But, in 1934, its methods and its number of members remained modest, and rivalries between its leaders crippled its power to act.

I watched this clearly unavoidable development with horror. It was plain that Austria was moving toward civil war. I could do nothing to prevent it. Even my best friends were of the opinion that the threat posed by the Social Democratic Party could only be opposed by violence.

The emergence of the Home Guard introduced a new type into politics: adventurers without education and desperados with limited perspectives ascended the ranks because they were good at drill and had command of loud voices. The manual of arms was their Bible, "authority" their slogan. They identified democracy with Social Democracy and therefore saw in it "the worst of all evils." Later, they clung to the catchword "Ständestaat," or "corporate state." Their social ideal was a military state in which they alone could give orders.

With the collapse of the *Bodenkreditanstalt* in May of 1931, the third phase of my activity with the *Handelskammer* came to a close. A limited scope of activity was all that remained available to me. I summoned all of my strength to fight the inflationary policy that had again been taken up by the government. That the inflation went no further than to the 175 Austrian shillings (up from 139 shillings) for 100 Swiss francs and that new stabilization at this rate of exchange resulted soon thereafter was my achievement alone.

But the fight for Austria remained lost. Even if I had achieved complete success, Austria could not have been saved. The enemy who was to destroy it came from the outside. Austria could not forever withstand the onrush of the National Socialists who were soon to overwhelm all of Europe.

Austria's problems were no longer domestic. Her fate lay in the hands of Western Europe. Anyone wanting to help Austria had to do so abroad. When I was offered the chair for "International Economic Relations" with Geneva's *Institut Universitaire de Hautes Etudes Internationales* in the spring of 1934, I accepted gladly. I retained my position with the *Handelskammer*, and returned to Vienna on occasion to continue in my old activity. But I was determined not to move back to Vienna until after the destruction of the National Socialist reich. I will return to my political activity as it developed between 1934 and 1938 in coming chapters.

I fought a battle in the *Handelskammer* for sixteen years in which I achieved nothing more than the postponement of catastrophe. I made weighty personal sacrifices, even though I always foresaw that I would be denied success. But I do not regret having attempted the impossible. I could not act otherwise. I fought because there was nothing else I could do.

9

My Teaching Activities in Vienna

No other calling was as desirable to me as that of a university professor. As a liberal, I recognized early on that I would always be denied a full professorship at a German-speaking university. This was regrettable to me only because it forced me to earn my living through nonacademic work. The title of *Privatdozent*[1] seemed to offer sufficient opportunity for salutary teaching.

In 1913 I was admitted to the faculty of law at the University of Vienna in the capacity of *Privatdozent*; in the spring of 1918 I received the title of "professor extraordinarius."[2] I made no further advances in my academic career in Austria. I am assuming that my name was dropped from the list of lecturers by the National Socialists in 1938, but they did not consider it worthy of their efforts to inform me.

---

[1]Unsalaried lecturer.

[2]A (full) professor who, in contrast to the "ordinary" or regular (full) professors, is not paid and has no chair (with a secretary, scientific assistants, and other employees) at the university.

I lectured during the early years of my academic career. I later limited myself to conducting a two-hour seminar on the problems of economic theory. Its success grew from year to year. Nearly all students who took the study of economics seriously attended my seminar. Admittedly, this was just a small percentage of the many hundreds of students who earned their doctorates in either law or the social sciences every year. But my seminars were overcrowded. A seminar does not customarily have more than 20–25 participants; mine regularly had 40–50.

After Wieser's retirement and Grünberg's move to Frankfurt, the three professorships in economics were held by Othmar Spann, Hans Mayer, and Count Ferdinand Degenfeld-Schonburg. Spann was barely acquainted with modern economics; he did not teach economics. Instead he preached universalism, that is, National Socialism. Degenfeld was more poorly versed in the problems of economics; the level of his instruction would have barely sufficed at a trade school of low rank. Mayer was Wieser's favorite pupil. He knew the works of Wieser and also those of Böhm and Menger. But he himself was without a facility for criticism, had never expressed an original thought, and had never really grasped what economics was all about. The awareness of his sterility and lack of creativity depressed him gravely and caused him to be unstable and malicious. He occupied his time with an open war against Spann and with spiteful intrigues directed against me. His lectures were miserable, and his seminar was not much better. It was not my imagination that the students, young doctors, and the numerous foreigners who studied in Vienna for a semester or two preferred my instruction.

Spann and Mayer were jealous of my success, and tried to alienate my students from me. My students claimed that they were treated uncommonly badly during examinations; I was not able to prove the accuracy of this claim. But I did make it clear to the students in my seminar that I placed no importance on their being officially registered. They made wide use of this allowance. Of the forty to fifty who attended, an average of only eight to ten was formally enrolled. The professors also made it difficult for doctoral candidates in the social sciences who wanted to write their dissertations with me. Those seeking the *Habilitation*[3] had to take special care not to be known as students of mine.

Students who had registered for my seminar were denied access to the library of the economics department unless they had registered for a seminar offered by one of the three professors as well. These measures fell entirely short of their purpose. I had seen to it that the library of the *Handelskammer* had been outfitted with a premier book collection. Modern Anglo-Saxon literature, in particular, was better represented there than it was in the university library.

I could not be bothered by all of these things. More serious was the low level of instruction at the University of Vienna in general. The splendor which had surrounded the university during my student years had long disappeared. Many professors could hardly be called educated men. A spirit foreign to culture and science presided over the faculties of the school of law and the school of humanities. In the first half of the 1920s, I was often invited to meetings with leading professors, the subject matter being the increase in state budget appropriations for the university. I was invited to these meetings because they counted on my recommendation to the financial counselor, Herr Patzauer, an associate of Commissioner Zimmerman. A letter written by a foreign friend of the Viennese culture was read during one of the meetings. In it, the terms "pragmatism," "behaviorism," and "revival," appeared. It became apparent that no one present had ever heard these expressions. On another occasion, it became clear that Benedette Croce's name was unknown to *all*, and that of Henri Bergson was unknown to most. Among the participants in these meetings were the president of the Academy

[3]Postdoctoral lecture qualification.

of Sciences, Oswald Redlich, a professor of medieval history, and Count Wenzel Gleisbach, of professor of criminal law.

One can thus imagine the average educational level of students. I administered the examinations in economics and finance in the state's master examinations in the social sciences. The ignorance displayed by the candidates was devastating. More vexing was the fact that the members of the examination committee did not take this failure seriously. I remember having a hard time persuading the committee to fail a candidate who believed that Marx had lived in the eighteenth century, and that the tax on beer was a direct tax. The same student also revealed in his examination in public law, among other things, that the idea of "ministerial accountability" was unknown to him. I would of course one day learn that this kind of ignorance could also be encountered in the highest of places. Austria's president, Miklas, who had been a secondary school history teacher, once participated in a discussion on the "most favored nation" clause with me and Professor Richard Reisch, the then president of the National Bank. In the course of the discussion I mentioned the Peace of Frankfurt. Miklas inquired as to when and between which countries this treaty had been signed.

There existed in Austria an unbridgeable divide between the vanishingly small group of Viennese intellectuals and the masses of so-called educated people. The educational system had taken such a deep downward turn that it no longer offered young people an education. The majority of doctors of law, of the social sciences, and of philosophy was inadequately trained in their professions, could not think, and was careful to avoid serious books. Of one hundred Viennese attorneys, ten, at the most, could read a journal in English or French. The proportion was much smaller outside of Vienna and among jurists in public service.

I brushed up against these conditions as an official with the *Handelskammer*. As a teacher I had dealt only with a select group of the most gifted. Even from 1906 to 1912, when I taught economics to the senior class of the Vienna Commercial Academy for Girls, and during the 1918/1919 academic year, when I offered a course for officers who sought reentry into civilian life at the Vienna Export Academy (later the Institute for World Trade), I dealt primarily with above-average students.

The main emphasis of my teaching activity lay in my *Privatseminar*. Beginning in 1920, I took care to gather a number of young people around myself every two weeks from October to June. My office in the *Handelskammer* was spacious enough to accommodate twenty to twenty-five persons. We usually met at seven in the evening and adjourned at ten thirty. In these gatherings we debated, without restraint, the important problems of economics, social philosophy, sociology, logic, and the epistemology of the sciences of human action. Within this circle the younger Austrian School of economics thrived. Within this circle Viennese culture experienced one of its last flowerings.

Here, I was neither teacher nor seminar leader. I was merely a *primus inter pares*,[4] who received more than gave.

Everyone belonging to the circle came voluntarily, guided only by his drive for knowledge. They came as students, but over the course of the years became friends. Later, even some of my contemporaries joined the circle. Foreign scholars visiting Vienna were welcome guests and eagerly took part in the goings on.

The *Privatseminar* had no official standing or function whatsoever. It was connected to neither the university nor the *Handelskammer*. It was and remained forever the circle of my much younger friends. Outsiders knew nothing of our gatherings; they saw only the published works of individual participants.

We cultivated neither school, nor community, nor sect. It was through contradiction rather than agreement that we supported each other. But in one thing we were united: in the desire to

---

[4]First among peers.

further the sciences of human action. Each was free to go the way his own law guided him. We never organized or took on anything resembling the foul "goings on" of the imperial and postwar German "scientists." We never considered publishing a journal or collection of works. Each did his own work, as is befitting a thinker. Still, each one of us labored for the circle, seeking no reward other than the recognition—not the applause—of friends.

There was greatness in this unpretentious exchange of ideas; in it we all found happiness and satisfaction.

Beside the *Privatseminar*, there was yet a second association of friends of economic inquiry. Since March 12, 1908, Karl Pribram, Emil Perels, Else Cronbach and I had held regular gatherings dedicated to the discussion of economic problems and fundamental questions in related fields. Before long, the circle grew. The lovely conference *Handelskammer of the Zentralstelle für Wohnungsreform*[5] provided a dignified setting. When I was away from Vienna during the war, the admission of new members was handled carelessly. The harmony of the proceedings had been disturbed, and by the time I returned home, gatherings had ceased. Immediately after the war I sought to revive the group. In order to avoid coming into conflict with the authorities, however, we had to establish a formal association, which we called the *Nationalökonomische Gesellschaft*[6]. A short while later we began having difficulties yet again and it became clear that cooperation with Spann was not possible. In time we succeeded in excluding Spann, and the society was able to resume its activities.

Anyone demonstrating genuine interest in economic problems could be elected to membership in the society. We held evening meetings at irregular intervals in the conference room

---

[5]Central Association for Housing Reform.

[6]Economic Society.

of the banking association, where society members and out-of-town guests gave lectures, always followed by lively discussion. The nucleus of the society's membership was formed by participants of my *Privatseminar*; but standing alongside these were a set of outstanding economists such as Richard Schüller, Siegfried Strakosch von Feldringen, Victor Graetz, and many others.

As the *Gesellschaft* did not want to be an affront to university professors, it felt it necessary to make Hans Mayer its president. I, myself, was vice president. When I left for Geneva in 1934, after which I only returned to Vienna for short visits, the *Gesellschaft* slowly began to fade away.

On March 19, 1938, Hans Mayer wrote to all members issuing notice that all non-Aryan members were to take leave of the *Nationalökonomische Gesellschaft*, "in consideration of the changed circumstances in German Austria, and in view of the respective laws now also applicable to this state."

This was the last that was heard of the society.

List of regular *Privatseminar* participants.

- Ludwig Bettelheim-Gabillon
- Victor Bloch
- Martha Stefanie Braun (Stephanie Browne)
- Friedrich Engel von Janosi
- Walter Fröhlich
- Gottfried von Haberler
- Friedrich A. von Hayek
- Marianne von Herzfeld
- Felix Kaufmann
- Rudolf Klein
- Helene Lieser-Berger
- Rudolf Löbl
- Gertrud Lovasy
- Fritz Machlup
- Ilse Mintz-Schüller
- Oskar Morgenstern
- Elly Offenheimer-Spiro
- Adolf G. Redlich-Redley
- Paul N. Rosenstein-Rodan
- Karol Schlesinger
- Fritz Schreier
- Alfred Schütz
- Richard von Strigl
- Erich Vögelin (Eric Voegelin)
- Robert Waelder
- Emanuel Winternitz

10

Scientific Work in Germany

I participated as a silent observer in meetings of the *Verein für Sozialpolitik*[1] held in Vienna in 1909 and Nürnberg in 1911. I was elected a member of the committee at its 1919 meeting in Regensburg. This did not mean a great deal; it was the honor customarily bestowed upon all who had contributed to the association's publications. But in time my position within the association became more meaningful. In contrast to its policy before the war, the association sought representation from all directions. Recognized as the representative of the Austrian School, I became ever more engaged. And so it happened that I was elected, in the end, to the board of directors. I took part in the preparation of the publications concerning the cartel problem. The preparation for and the staging of the debates on the problem of economic value held in Dresden in 1932 were predominantly my work.

I was elected—I believe it was in 1924 or 1925—a member of the *Deutsche Gesellschaft für Soziologie*[2].

---

[1]Association for Social Policy.

[2]German Sociological Society.

I withdrew from both organizations in 1933.

I was not favorably impressed with German professors of economic state sciences and sociology. There were among them a number of educated and sincere men filled with genuine scientific aspirations. But most of them were not.

That these men were not economists, and in fact, that they usually assumed stances opposed to economics, should not be held against them. They were, after all, the students of Schmoller, Wagner, Bücher, and Brentano. They did not know the economics literature and had only the scantest idea of economic problems. Every economist was suspected of being an enemy of the state, anti-German, and a protagonist of business interests and free trade. And whenever they actually picked up an economics essay, they wanted, most emphatically, to discover its errors and deficiencies. They were dilettantes in all that they undertook. They wanted to be historians, but they scarcely looked at the interdisciplinary sciences, the most important tools of the historian. A spirit of historical research was alien to them. They were unacquainted with the basic questions of statistics. They were laymen in jurisprudence, technology, banking, and trade. They published books and essays concerning things they knew nothing about with amazing carelessness.

What was much worse was that they were always ready to move with the shifting winds. In 1918 most of them sympathized with the Social Democrats; in 1933 they made agreements with the Nazis. They would have become communists had the Bolshevists come to the fore.

Werner Sombart was the great master of this set. He is said to be a pioneer in economic history, economic theory, and sociology; he was deemed an upstanding man because he had once aroused the anger of Kaiser Wilhelm. The recognition of his colleagues was well earned by Sombart, as he combined in his person all of their shortcomings to the highest degree. He had never known any ambition other than to make money and to attract attention to himself. His sizable work on modern capitalism is a historical bungling. He had always speculated on public applause alone, writing paradoxes to guarantee success. He was unusually gifted, but never sought serious thought and endeavor. He took his part in suffering from delusions of grandeur, the occupational disease of German professors. He professed Marxism when doing so was fashionable; when Hitler came to power, he wrote that the führer received his orders from God.

He had no interest in economics whatsoever. In about 1922, when he was asked by Weiss-Wellenstein, in my presence, if he wished to give a lecture on inflation, he declined with the words: "That problem is a technical one of banks. Having nothing to do with economics, it does not interest me." His original title for his book, *The Three Economies*, was *The End of Economics*. He told me that he had rejected this title out of regard for his colleagues who made their livings teaching economics.

Nevertheless, it was more interesting to talk with Sombart than with most of the other professors. At least he was not stupid or limited.

Many professors claimed to be specialists in theory. Among these were Gottl and Oppenheimer, monomaniacs too big for their own boots; Diehl was a narrow-minded ignoramus; and Spiethoff was a man never able to publish a book.

At the helm of the *Verein* during those years was Professor Eckhart, a likeable Rhinelander who produced nothing of significance with the exception of a few contributions to the history of German domestic maritime commerce. His rival was Bernhard Harms, who had popularized the term *Weltwirtschaft*[3] in Germany. Driven by his desire to assume leadership of an organization, he founded the *List-Gesellschaft*.[4]

---

[3]Global economy.

[4]The Friedrich List Society, 1925–1934.

Keeping company with these men made it clear to me that the German people could no longer be saved; these characterless imbeciles were already an elite few, chosen from the best. The field they taught at the universities was the most critical to a political education. The educated, as well as the masses, treated them as ambassadors of the science. What was to become of a youth with such teachers?

In 1918, in Vienna, Max Weber said to me,

> You don't like the *Verein*. I like it even less, but at this time, it is the only such association of men in our field. Criticism from outside does not help. One must work within the association itself and seek to remedy its shortcomings. I will try in my way, and you must do it in yours.

I heeded Weber's advice, though I knew that it would be in vain. As an Austrian, as a *Privatdozent*, and as a "theorist," I remained an outsider to the *Verein*. I was treated with the utmost courtesy, but I was seen as a stranger.

Even Max Weber could do nothing to alter the situation. The early death of this genius was a great disaster for Germany. Had Weber lived longer, the German people of today would be able to look to this example of an "Aryan" who would not be broken by National Socialism. But even such an intellect could do nothing to change the course of fate.

I also met men in both of these German societies whose company enriched me greatly. I recall, above all, Max Scheler, the philosopher and sociologist. Then there were Leopold von Wiese, the sociologist from Cologne; Moriz Bohm; and Albert Hahn from Frankfurt. I met Walter Sulzbach and his wife, Maria Sulzbach-Fürth, at the 1926 meeting of the *Deutsche Gesellschaft für Soziologie* in Vienna. I have pursued a friendship with them for years. I would also like to mention others, namely, Wilhelm Röpke, Alexander Rüstow, Götz Briefs, Georg Halm, and Richard Passow. The subtly minded historian Eberhard

Gothein and the penetrating and upstanding Ludwig Pohle have, unfortunately, already passed away.

There was talk of a possible appointment for me at a German university on two occasions: in 1925 at the University of Kiel, and in 1928 (or was it 1927?) at the *Handelshochschule Berlin*.[5] The etatists and the socialists unleashed a passionate agitation against me both times and the appointments failed to materialize. I had not expected anything other. I was ill-suited to teaching Prussia's royal police science.

[5]The Berlin School of Commerce.

11

Further Studies in Indirect Exchange

I was not satisfied with a number of things in *The Theory of Money and Credit*. I found it necessary to remedy its shortcomings.

Neither the criticism of my book, nor the works of others published on the problems of indirect exchange since 1911 were in any way able to shake my claims. I am grateful for the incentive provided by the works of B.M. Anderson, T.E. Gregory, D.H. Robertson, Albert Hahn, Hayek, and Machlup. They caused me to reconsider my theory and improve its presentation. Even where they opposed my reasoning, they confirmed rather than rejected the core of my teaching. From the writings of these men I gained not only an education, but found in them as well the comfort that I was not on my own as an economist, working for the sake of libraries alone.

Surely enough, the rest of the publications on the problems of money and credit published in the last thirty years were rather insignificant. The decline in scientific thinking was shocking. One can say that some of the works appearing during this time were acceptable in general, even though some things seemed untenable and there were deficiencies with regard to presentation.

Indeed, the majority of the books and articles are completely worthless.

Such harsh judgment applies principally to works that claim to point out "errors" that are contradicted or remain unexplained by "orthodox" theories. With but little understanding of the history of money and banking, the authors see these errors as new and unprecedented. They do not attempt to explain the facts in light of "orthodox" theory, because knowledge of the same and the ability to think scientifically escapes them.

I believe that keeping up with the literature day to day and providing solid critique for every nonsensical and insignificant assertion was an important job. Of course this would not prevent the repetition of old errors, but one could do a great service to the public interested in economic questions. Some friends and I pondered the launching of a new publication with this as its aim. But we were unable to find a publisher willing to take on the project without the assurance of financial subsidy.

What's more, I am of the opinion that the refutation of current errors has much to offer as a topic for doctoral theses by the younger practitioners of our science. In fact, the minimal requirement of an economist is that he be able to recognize fallacies and refute them critically. I have encouraged works of this type on occasion.

There is only one such thesis I would like to mention here, one whose publication was prevented due to the difficult conditions prevailing in Austria in 1920. This is the work that earned Helene Lieser the first doctorate in the social sciences ever conferred upon a woman by an Austrian university. The dissertation dealt with the currency reform programs advanced in Austria during the years of the bank-note depreciation. She demonstrated that most of the reform proposals discussed in European countries in 1920 were not as new as their authors would have had us believe.

In my seminar, I seized every opportunity to refute popular errors. Indeed, I had neither the time nor the intent to dedicate my polemic efforts to falsities that had already been refuted a hundred times. I rather regret having spent too much of my limited strength in the war against pseudoeconomics. In hours of quiet reflection I repeatedly renewed my resolve to be guided by the passage of Spinoza: *veritas norma sui et falsi est*.[1] But time and again I let myself be carried away by my temperament.

I published many articles during the inflation that were intended to explain the nature of monetary depreciation and refute the balance-of-payment theory of exchange rates. In addition to the article on quantity theory just mentioned, I wrote "Zahlungsbilanz und Devisenkurs"[2] for the *Mitteilungen des Vereins Österreichischer Banken und Bankiers*,[3] a journal that has in the meantime become available to the public.

For the *Schriften des Vereins für Sozialpolitik* I wrote "Geldtheorie Seit des Stabiliserungsproblems."[4] This essay was held in abeyance for many months by the board members of the *Verein*: they found questionable its rejection of the official thesis that the depreciation of the mark was caused by reparation payments and the French occupation. It was not published until the summer of 1923, my second article appearing in the journal. In 1919 I had contributed an essay to a volume on annexation problems of the reentry of German Austria into the German Empire and the currency problem.

---

[1]*Sane sicut lux se ipsam et tenebras manifestat, sic veritas norma sui et falsi est* (Latin). Translation: "Indeed, just as light defines itself and darkness, so truth sets the standard for itself and falsity."

[2]"Balance of Payments and Foreign Exchange Rates."

[3]The official journal of the Association of Austrian Bankers.

[4]Translation: "The Stabilization of the Monetary Unit from the viewpoint of theory."

In the second edition of *The Theory of Money and Credit* and in the small publication "Geldwertstabilisierung und Konjunkturpolitik"[5] I framed the lessons on the trade cycle in a way that explained the cycle completely. The boom is facilitated by credit expansion. But what causes credit expansion? I had not answered this question in the first edition. Since that time I had found the answer. Banks want to lower the interest rate through credit expansion. Monetary policy that favors "cheap money" and the notion that credit expansion is the suitable means for attaining interest reduction encourages this practice and attempts to create the institutional conditions necessary for it.

Writing my *Nationalökonomie* afforded me the opportunity to think through my theory of money and credit yet again and present it in a new form.

In my book on money I had directed my critique at the widely accepted concept of direct exchange without use of money only inasmuch as it was necessary to reject the doctrine of the neutrality of money. I had only dealt with the problems of monetary calculation as was necessary for my inquiry into the social consequences of monetary depreciation. Anything further was to be left to the theory of direct exchange. But the basic thought was introduced in the book on money: there are values and valuations, to be sure, but no measurements of value and no value calculations; the market economy calculates with money prices. This was not new; it was that which flowed logically from the theory of subjective value. Gossen had already hinted at the conclusions that could thereby be drawn for the theory of a socialist economy. Pierson, whose work I came to know many years later through Hayek's translation, had repeated Gossen's thought.

When I set out to work on my book, *Socialism*, I was compelled to place special emphasis on the fundamentals of catallactics. A theory of socialism not having a consideration of the

---

[5]Translated: "Monetary Stabilization and Cyclical Policy."

problem of economic calculation at its very foundation would be simply absurd. In 1919, therefore, I wrote and presented the *Nationalökonomisch Gesellschaft* with the essay, "Die Wirtschaftsrechnung im sozialistischen Gemeinwesen."[6] At the suggestion of friends, I published it in 1920 in *Archiv für Sozialwissenschaft und Sozialpolitik*.[7] It is incorporated in *Socialism* in an essentially unaltered form.

All attempts at disproving the conclusiveness of my thesis were destined for failure because they did not penetrate the value theory at the core of the problem. All of these books, theses, and essays tried to rescue socialism. They wanted to show that it was indeed possible to construct a socialist commonwealth in which economic calculations could be performed. They failed to see that one must begin with the question of how in an economy consisting of preferring or deferring–that is, making unequal valuations–one can arrive at comparable valuations and the use of equations. So it was that they came upon the absurd idea of recommending the equations of mathematical catallactics, which depict an image devoid of human action, as a substitute for the monetary calculation of the market economy.

It was in *Socialism* that I finally had the opportunity to present the problems of economic calculation in all of its significance. In the meantime I had to content myself with demonstrating the errors and contradictions of theretofore proposed suggestions for socialist economic calculation. It was only in the explanations put forth in the third part of *Socialism* that my theory of money (1940) found completion. Thus did I carry out the plan I had conceived thirty-five years earlier; I combined the theory of indirect exchange with the theory of direct exchange into a unified system of human action.

---

[6]"Economic Calculation in the Socialist Commonwealth."

[7]"Archives for Social Sciences and Politics."

12

Systems of Social Cooperation

The impossibility of economic calculation in a socialist economy is the theory at the core of my book, *Gemeinwirtschaft*,[1] whose first edition appeared in 1922. *Gemeinwirtschaft, Liberalismus*,[2] published in 1927, and the 1929 compilation of articles that appeared under the title *Kritik des Interventionismus*[3] together offer a comprehensive analysis of the problems of social cooperation. In these volumes, I investigate all conceivable systems of cooperation and examine their feasibility. These studies found closure in *Nationalökonomie*.[4] I had intended to include yet another essay in the collection, *Kritik des Interventionismus*, namely, "Die Verstaatlichung des Kredits,"[5]

[1]*Socialism*.

[2]*Liberalism*.

[3]*Critique of Interventionism*.

[4]It appeared nine years later as *Human Action*.

[5]"The Nationalization of Credit."

which had appeared in the *Zeitschrift für Nationalökonomie* in 1929. The *Zeitschrift*'s editors, however, mislaid the essay, and rediscovered it only after the collection had gone to press.

I believe that the theories presented in these volumes are irrefutable. I had introduced a new perspective in the handling of these problems, the only one that made possible a scientific discussion of political questions. I made inquiry into the usefulness of proposed measures, that is, whether the objective that the use of these measures was intended to achieve could actually be obtained through the means recommended and employed. I showed that the evaluation of the various systems of social cooperation is ineffective when conducted from arbitrarily chosen points of view.

It is another thing entirely to assert that the evolution of the system of private property in the means of production inevitably leads to socialism or interventionism. Even if this were true, it would not disprove my claims. Neither socialism nor interventionism gain meaning or purpose from the assertion that history inevitably leads to them. When the "return to capitalism" is ruled out, as is generally maintained, then the fate of our civilization is sealed. But I demonstrated that the theory of the inescapability of socialism and interventionism is untenable. Capitalism does not destroy itself. People wish to do away with it because it is in socialism or interventionism that they behold salvation.

From time to time I entertained the hope that my writings would bear practical fruit and point policy in the right direction. I have always looked for evidence of a change in ideology. But I never actually deceived myself; my theories explain, but cannot slow the decline of a great civilization. I set out to be a reformer, but only became the historian of decline.

In my works on social cooperation, I have spent much time and effort disputing socialists and interventionists of all varieties and trends. The matter at hand—the repudiation of contrary-to-purpose reforms—made the effort necessary.

I was charged with not having considered the psychological aspect of the problem of cooperation. After all, man has a soul. This soul is said to find itself uneasy in a capitalist system, and it would be willing to suffer a reduction in living standards in exchange for a society with a more satisfactory labor and employment structure.

Firstly, it is important to establish that this argument (we will call it the *heart argument*) is not compatible with what we will call the *head argument*, the original argument of the socialists and interventionists, and the one they still hold today. The head argument justifies socialist programs by asserting that capitalism hinders the full development of productive capabilities. Socialist methods would increase output immeasurably, thereby creating conditions that make ample provisions possible for all. Marxism is founded on the head argument entirely. Before Lenin, the Marxists never affirmed that the transition to socialism would lower the standard of living during the transition period. They announced immediate improvement in the material situation of the masses, here and there adding that the full blessings of socialist production methods would be manifest only in time. As a result of criticism wielded against socialist programs, the heart argument is the one socialists were compelled to enlist in fighting for their cause.

In judging the heart argument, of course, of decisive importance is the extent of the reduction in economic well-being brought about by a socialist production system. Since this cannot be ascertained objectively or measured precisely, the argument between the adherents and opponents of socialism is said to be scientifically insoluble; economics cannot resolve the conflict.

I took a turn in dealing with the problem that does not allow for the application of the heart argument. If a socialist system leads to chaos because it is a system wherein economic calculation is impossible, and if interventionism cannot attain the objectives desired by its proponents, then coming to the aid of these illogical systems through the heart argument is irrelevant.

I have never denied that emotional factors explain the popularity of anticapitalist policies. But inexpedient proposals and measures cannot be made expedient by factors of this type. If people cannot tolerate capitalism "psychologically," then the culture of capitalism will fail.

I have been charged with overestimating the roles played by logic and reason in life. In theory there is no *either/or*. Life, I was told, consists of compromises. What appears incompatible in scientific analysis sometimes takes a feasible shape in praxis; politics will find a way of blending conflicting principles. The solution may well be called illogical, irrational, and senseless, but it can be fruitful. This alone is what matters.

The critics are mistaken. People wish to follow through on that which they deem suitable. Nothing is more remote to them than a half-realized desire. Here man makes no appeal to historical experience. It is true that those religions that call for a turning away from earthly concerns have gotten along quite well in this world. But the rigorous teachings of Christianity and Buddhism have never tamed the spirits. The stringent teachings of these two religions that have crossed over into the popular faith have not stood in the way of the activities of secular life. Compliance to religious commands was reserved for the monks. Even during the Middle Ages, princes of the Church did not allow their activities to be influenced by consideration of the commands of the Sermon on the Mount and other evangelical teachings. The small band of those who actually took Christianity and Buddhism seriously retreated from worldly affairs. The lives of those remaining were not a compromise, but simply un-Christian and un-Buddhist.

Today we face a problem of a different kind. The masses tend toward socialism or interventionism; in any case, they are anticapitalistic. But the individualist does not seek to rescue his soul from the world; he wants to refashion the world. He will see things through to the end. The masses are implacable in their consistency: they would rather destroy the world than be robbed of one iota of their agenda.

There is no consolation in recalling the fact that there had always been interventionism in the precapitalist past. Far fewer people lived on the earth's surface then, and the masses were content with living conditions they would today find intolerable. One cannot simply withdraw from capitalism and return to a century gone by.

13

Epistemological Studies

Throughout the course of the nineteenth century, and upon the ruins of old religious beliefs, various sects began to entrench themselves; they sought to offer their followers a "substitute" for lost faith. The most lasting of these sects is positivism, the "incongruous insistence of bad science and eviscerated papistry," as Huxley called it (*Collected Essays*, vol. V). In reaction against church practices, positivism found many ardent disciples in Catholic countries. Vienna was the city of Saint Clemens Maria Hofbauer, a positivist who believed himself to be truly free and free of prejudice, and his "Griesknödel"[1] miracle.

Positivism is usually credited with the development of sociology. That the term "sociology" was coined by August Comte is correct. But that which is pursued under the name of sociology,

[1] Or "Grießknoedel," a farina dumpling commonly eaten in Germany and Austria with fruit or in broth. Hofbauer is known for his early work in a bakery monastery, where he labored day and night to feed the poor.

insofar as it is not just idle talk, has nothing to do with a positivist program of a science of human action built upon experience with the methods of Newtonian physics. Comte's sociology is one of ethnography, cultural history, and psychology, and makes use of the old methods of history. He wanted nothing to do with the science of human action whose history began in classical economics. In this his followers remained faithful to their master.

For some time German universities rejected positivism and their doors remained closed to sociology. This enmity had little to do with scientific deliberation; it was of a political nature. When the positivists began to experience success, the German sciences had already assumed a hostile position toward western thought. Positivism was rejected because it came from France. But attitudes toward positivism's central point wavered. It is notable that the historicism of the Schmoller School held to the belief that the laws of economics were to be derived from experiences in recorded economic history.

One can also say that the last great effort of German epistemology was made in dealing with problems not raised by positivism, but those that it made controversial. The building blocks of the theory of scientific understanding in the humanities were laid by scholars whose writings predated Comte, or who did not know him. Its development was a reaction against positivism, and no less against the historical materialism of the Marxists.

It followed that I saw no possibilities for economic science when I entered the university. I was convinced that economic history must make use of the means and methods of the historical disciplines and could never yield economic laws. I believed that there was nothing in economic life that could be made the object of scientific analysis outside of economic history. There could not have been a more consistent follower of historicism than I.

The cohesiveness of my epistemology suffered an irreparable breach after I actually came to know economics. I was helpless.

The writings of the *Methodenstreit*[2]—even Menger's splendid work—did not satisfy me. I was even more disappointed by John Stuart Mill. It was not until many years later that I became acquainted with Cairnes and Senior.

I tried to console myself with the fact that what mattered was the furthering of science and that problems of methodology were of lesser importance. I soon recognized the error of this stance. With each problem, the economist confronts the basic questions: whence do these principles come, what is their significance, and how do they relate to experience and "reality"? These are not problems of method or even research technique; they are themselves the fundamental questions. Can one construct a system of deduction without having asked the questions upon which the system is to be built?

I searched in vain for enlightenment in the writings of the Lausanne and Anglo-Saxon schools. Even there I encountered the same uncertainty and wavering between irreconcilable points of view. That these conditions led to the demise of economic thought came as no surprise. Institutionalism, on the one hand, and the empty dogmatism of the mathematical school, on the other, is the result.

I hesitated for a long time in making my investigations into these fundamental questions publicly known; I was aware that they reached far beyond the field of economics. In fact, the matter at hand was the opening up of a new field of epistemology and logic.

Until now, logic and epistemology have only addressed the thinking associated with experience and the natural sciences, and with the deductive system of mathematics. History, by comparison, was simply "not science." Economics, at first, was not

---

[2]Controversy over method and epistemology in economics in the 1880s and 1990s. The two leading figures were Carl Menger and Gustav Schmoller.

considered a science at all. When it finally became necessary to include it, one was content to assert that the discipline dealt with the economic aspects of human action. Aside from the fact that this *homo oeconomicus* is inapplicable to the subjective value theory, it does not solve the question of the origins of the knowledge of purely economic behavior.

Identifying the idiosyncrasies of the historical method was enormous progress, as was the development of the theories of *Verstehen* and *ideal types*. The fact that infamous metaphysicians sought refuge under the roof of these new theories does not detract from the value of their discovery. No architect is held responsible for the behavior of those who inhabit the structure he designed. What is more critical is that a man of Max Weber's rank also sought to cast economic principles according to his model of ideal types.

I developed my theory in a series of critical essays, the first of which appeared in 1928. These essays were compiled in 1933 and published in one volume under the title *Grundprobleme der Nationalökonomie*.[3] The opening essay was one that had not before appeared in print. I summarized this material yet again in *Nationalökonomie*.

In the essay originally published in 1928, I sought to eliminate the distinction between economic and noneconomic action. The subjective value theory had already brought about deliverance from this specter, but Menger and Böhm-Bawerk had not drawn all necessary conclusions given their basic position.

The next essay, appearing under the title "Sociology and History," was concerned with the investigation of the theoretical science of human action and of history. Here I made the mistake of using the term "sociology" to designate the theory of human action. I should have used the term "praxeology." That which

[3] *Epistemological Problems of Economics*.

one generally calls sociology today is not theoretical, but historical knowledge. Max Weber was quite right in describing what he saw to be sociology in terms of the humanities. He observed that this was the sociology that worked with the formation of ideal types. His error lay in assigning to it many praxeological elements and in seeing economics as a field serviced by the intellectual methods of understanding. My essay was primarily directed against Max Weber's epistemology, about which I raised two objections: its failure to comprehend the epistemological characteristics of economics, and its distinction between rational actions and actions oriented otherwise.

In a third essay I contrasted understanding in the historical disciplines with comprehending in economics and praxeology. Lastly, in the essay that serves as an introduction in *Grundprobleme der Nationalökonomie,* I demonstrated the *a priori* nature of praxeological knowledge. It was thus that I drew the epistemological conclusion from the scientific development that began with the discovery of regularity in market phenomena in the eighteenth century.

I was fully aware that my theory would meet with rejection at first. I knew the positivist bias of my contemporaries rather well. The reigning panphysicalism is blind to the basic problems of epistemology, looking even upon the biological problems as "disturbances" of its worldview. To these fanatics, everything else is senseless metaphysics flirting with pseudoproblems. One cannot make excuses for the excesses of this neopositivism by recalling at the same time the no-less-regrettable fabrications of idealistic philosophy, or even by considering it a "beneficial" reaction. It is indeed the task of the historian of dogma to understand error and thereby explain it. Understanding cannot, however, provide an argument toward a more satisfactory solution in answer to error. I believe I understand positivism, but this has nothing to do with whether or not its answers are useful.

It is clear to me that it would be impossible to unsettle, much less extirpate the popularity of, positivist metaphysics with an explanation of the epistemological characteristics of the science of human action. Economic problems, unlike those of biology and physics, are much too complex to be entrusted to the abilities of the multitudes as part of a program of general education. Positivism has made classical physics palatable to the masses, and neopositivism has done the same for the present state of physical teachings. Both adulterate and simplify in a manner similar to that in which Darwinism has been recast for everyday usage with the cliché "man is descended from apes." Much time will elapse before people dispense with such raw simplifications. Until then, the bourgeoisie will remain occupied with a popular philosophy.

Whether or not the small number of thinkers will be satisfied with the system of empiricism is another question. I do not wish to take into account that this system simply refuses to acknowledge the science of human action, and therefore, contrary to its own emphatically asserted principle, rejects what does not fit into its system. But can man get along with positivist assertions about logical principles in the long run?

The principles of logic are said to be arbitrarily chosen conventions that have proven themselves practical or useful. Viewed in this way, one is only postponing the problem without bringing it any closer to resolution. One may claim that man has tried various arbitrarily chosen rules and, in the end, has held fast to those that have proven themselves effective. But in terms of what purpose did these rules appear effective? If this is the question posed, then one has arrived again at the problem of intellectual mastery of worldly things, and at the problems of explication and truth. For this reason it is also futile to attempt to solve the problems of truth through an appeal to usefulness.

Since these principles of logic were arrived at arbitrarily, could one just as easily have chosen other principles, if their effectiveness were the same in terms of purpose? No, certainly not. The basic relations used by logic to link statements are necessary to and inseparable from human thought; irreconcilable relations are unimaginable. The category of negation is not arbitrarily chosen; it is necessary to thought. No thought can dispense with it. Even if we wanted to assume that the distinction between yes and no were a product won by experience, or that once arbitrarily established proved itself through experience, one has not yet refuted the contention that, logically, the ability to comprehend yes and no must precede all thought.

The basic assumptions of logic have been called the rules of the game. But what must be added is that this game is our life: we are born into this game and must play as long as we live; for man there is no second game with a different set of rules.

Praxeology's special calling is to reveal the fallacies of conventionalism, as it does not adhere to the cult of the word "purpose." The purpose of action is to attain success in the world that is our environment. Adjusting to the conditions of this world and its order is therefore expedient in any case. If the human mind can give birth to rules of the game that are useful in this adjustment, then only two explanations remain open: either there is something in our minds that belongs to the environment and permits us to understand it—an *a priori*; or the environment plies our minds with rules that enable us to deal with it. In no case is there room for arbitrariness and convention. Logic is either active within us or effected within us. It affects the world through us, or the world affects us through it. Logic is the stuff of the world, of reality, and of life.

It is not at all obvious what is to be achieved by doggedly contesting the *a priori*. Even if we were to assume that experience leads us to comprehension of the category of means and ends, the question remains open: what is in us that allows for experience at all, and indeed, such experience wherein a different outcome appears plainly absurd? What sense does it make to claim to have gained this knowledge through experience when we cannot boast of other outcomes to which other experiences could have led? When I say that experience has shown A to be red, it is meaningful in that our minds could have also recognized another outcome. But if it were said that experience had led us to the category of negation or that of means and ends? This is senseless; what, then, could other experiences have taught us?

The same is true of conventionalism. What other rules of the game could take the place of logical principles or the praxeological concept of action? One could play a game that differs from a standard game of chess in that one of its rules is replaced by another arbitrarily chosen one. But can one "play" with thinking that does not distinguish between yes and no? If this question is answered in the negative, then it is plain to see that the nature of this difference is one that deviates from the rules of the game. Here, again, we encounter the inescapable *a priori*.

We are not sketching a plan for a new economics when we assert that economics is a deductive system derived from an *a priori* point of departure. Rather, we are demonstrating what today's economics is.

It did not escape me, naturally, that there were also attempts to conduct economics as an experimental science. There is an economics association that adopted for its motto: "Science is measurement." With Menger, I will be happy to see this movement, richly endowed with financial support, run its full course. But it is not worthwhile to refute yet again the notion that in the sphere of human action measurements can be made in the same way they are made in physics. Economic statistics is a method of economic history, and not a method from which theoretical insight can be won.

Even in economic history, one must understand where comprehension is no longer sufficient. After all data have been acquired that have or could have affected an event to be researched, it is only with *Verstehen*[4] that one can begin to approach an answer to the questions of if and to what degree the

[4]The understanding and interpretation of the meaning of human action.

individual factors had an impact on the result. It is precisely in the quantitative that the task of "understanding," which allows for exactness or near exactness in the area of physics, lies in the sphere of human action: here there are no constant relations between quantities.

Mathematics and physics are undergoing a severe crisis from which they will emerge in a new form. Little remains of the cheerful trust in the indisputable certainty, clarity, and exactness of its tenets that once led them to look down with pity on the poor arts and ignore economics entirely. Mathematicians and physicists are now beginning—tardily enough—to acknowledge logical and epistemological problems. Logic and the epistemology of the science of human action cannot learn anything from physics and mathematics. But the "exact" sciences still have much to learn from their once-disdained siblings. The cleft between the natural sciences and the sciences of human action will thereby not be bridged. A unified science can be achieved only when the physical and chemical processes of physiology that generate the thought, "two times two are four," can be distinguished from those that generate the thought, "two times two are five."

My epistemological studies did more than serve the development of logic and epistemology, and disclose the errors of positivism, irrationalism, and historicism.

I dealt as well with polylogism.

14

My Teaching Activities in Geneva

After thirty years of service, my position with the *Handelskammer* entitled me to retire with a lifetime pension of nearly 15,000 shillings per year. Every *Handelskammer* official received double credit for two and a half years of war service. In addition, I received credit for three years of prewar service. Since a service year that had begun was counted as a full year, I had earned the right to enter into retirement on October 1, 1932. I had always awaited the coming of this date with mixed feelings. On the one hand, I wanted to shed the obligations of my office in order to dedicate myself fully to scientific work. On the other hand, I had to admit that the pension promised to me seemed downright precarious in light of the general uncertainty of conditions.

The apparatus of the *Handelskammer* had become greatly uncomfortable for all political parties. This was largely due to the economic activity that had unfolded as a result of my efforts. The *Handelskammer* had always been a thorn in the side of the Social Democrats. The *Großdeutschen* saw an obstacle to the Anschluss in the intellectual ascendancy of the Viennese *Handelskammer*. Within the Christian Social Party, the agrarian wing, largely under Dollfuss's leadership, had gained the upper hand. The agrarians saw in the *Handelskammer* the main opponent of their politics. The plan was to abolish the *Handelskammer* through special legislation in the course of the restructuring of economic society. The catchword "Ständestaat"[1] was quite meaningless in Austria. It did nothing but guard the aspirations of the Christian Socialist Party and its allied *Heimwehr*[2] in unchecked party rule. No one really knew enough to boast about what he imagined "Ständestaat" to mean. But everyone knew that the Chamber of Commerce, Handicrafts, and Industry was not a good fit for the Ständestaat, and as a liberal institution had best vanish.

Next to me there were only two officials in the *Handelskammer* who were in the position to fight for its preservation: Dr. Wilhelm Becker in Vienna, and Dr. Wilhelm Taucher in Graz, whose second job was that of an assistant professor at the University of Graz. In the fall of 1937 and during the first weeks of 1938 he was a member of Schuschnigg's cabinet. Both men found cause for concern in my entering into retirement and induced me to take up the *Handelskammer*'s cause and defend our pension claims. At stake here were only our own personal interests. The internal struggle for Austria had come to an end with the banking crisis having made banks, and thereby big industry, directly dependent on the central bank.

In the spring of 1934 I received, most unexpectedly, the invitation to assume the chair for international economic relations at the Institut Universitaire des Hautes Etudes Internationales in Geneva for the academic year 1934–35. I accepted immediately. I did not formally resign from the *Handelskammer*. I retained the direction of the *Handelskammer*'s department of

---

[1]Corporate state.

[2]Home guard.

finance and promised to return to Vienna as often as it should become necessary. But I gave up two-thirds of my salary during my absence.

When I went to Geneva in 1934, I assumed that my appointment was only for one academic year. But my contract was renewed; I stayed in Geneva until the end of the 1939–1940 academic year.

I sensed liberation in the distance from the daily routines in the *Handelskammer* and from the political duties that I could not have escaped in Vienna. I was finally able to concern myself fully and almost exclusively with scientific problems.

The institute was a creation of its directors, William E. Rappart and Paul Mantoux. The teaching load it imposed upon its faculty was minimal: one hour of lecture and two hours of seminar per week. An affectionate understanding reigned among teachers and students. The spirit of liberalism shone upon this unique institution.

That we were all fighting for a lost cause could not be mistaken. The flood of barbarism was rising around us.

The Geneva of those years will live on in history as the seat of the League of Nations. The League of Nations was never real. The diplomats had turned a great idea into a bureaucracy with several hundred employees. There were officials who had no interests other than retaining their positions. At the head of this bureaucracy was the unimaginative, small-minded French bureaucrat, M. Joseph Avenol. The officials were similar to their chief.

The League of Nations did not fail on account of the inability and indolence of its officials. It never came to life because it lacked the ideological foundation. In a liberal world, individual states and nations can cooperate peacefully without supranational organization. In a world pervaded by nationalism, neither treaties nor the creation of international agencies can eliminate conflict.

The failure of the League of Nations also paralyzed the development of the institute founded by Rapport and Mantoux.

Young people who frequented it came to Geneva with more than the purpose of attending lectures and seminars alone. In Geneva they wanted to escape the narrow nationalism of their home countries and engage the spirit of international cooperation. But what they saw of the League of Nations filled them with dismay and robbed them of their courage. They found the atmosphere in Geneva unbearable. As much as the institute appealed to them, they were disappointed by everything they experienced of "international" life.

The outbreak of the new war limited the activity of the institute considerably. Its only students now were the Swiss and political refugees awaiting the opportunity to emigrate to America. Because I could no longer bear living in a country that considered my presence a political burden and a threat to its security, I left the Institut in July of 1940.

15

The Struggle for Austria's Survival

When I went to Geneva I did not deceive myself about the hopelessness of Austria's fight for autonomy.

The politicians at the fore lacked the ability to fight this battle externally; foreign countries were completely unknown to them. They neither understood their languages, nor their mentalities or political outlook. They were not even in the position to furnish information to attested foreign diplomats and journalists in Vienna. While in Vienna, diplomats made a study of the pleasures of the *Heurigen*[1] and enjoyed winter sports. Business affairs were left to press consultants of the missions. The most active of these was the Italian Eugenio Morreale.

The government did not concern itself with foreign newspapermen at all. Providing information to these correspondents was left to the Social Democrats.

The complete lack of ability on the part of Social Democratic leaders had catastrophic effects. Otto Bauer had elevated the demand for unification with Germany to the party platform in

---

[1]*Heurigen* translates as both new wine (*heuer* meaning "this year"), and the establishment in which it is served.

1918. He based this on the notion that the authority of the proletariat was assured for all time in highly industrialized Germany. But in Austria, where the majority of the population was made up of farmers, farm workers, and craftsman, he feared defeat of the proletariat by the other classes. Bauer refused to alter his policies even when the National Socialists seized power in Germany. In his stubbornness, he failed to see that holding fast to an Anschluss program was grist in the mill of the Nazis.

The Social Democrats simply did not want to recognize that it was only the Italians who were ready to support Austria in its fight against the National Socialist takeover. They fought passionately against a "fascist" course of foreign policy. In January of 1934, Dollfuss was ready to surrender to the National Socialists. Negotiations were already quite advanced when, in the last minute, Italy put in its veto. "Il Duce" sent his undersecretary of state, Suvich, to Vienna to assure the government of his support. It was then that the Social Democrats added the crowning touch to their stupidity. Their journal, *The Labor Press,* accused Suvich of having deserted the Austrian Army in World War I. The Social Democrats organized turbulent street demonstrations against "Il Duce's" delegate. It was only through a massive contingent of police and the *Heimwehr* that Suvich was protected from personal injury. In order to make amends with Suvich, the government suspended the mailing of *The Labor Press* for one month. The Social Democrats answered with more intense demonstrations, which, in turn, resulted in the crushing of their leaders by government troops and the *Heimwehr*, and brought about an end to the rule of the Social Democratic Party in Viennese city government.

Leaders of the Social Democratic Party who had fled to London, Paris, and Prague now openly refused any support of Austria in her fight against Hitler. They felt there was no difference between Austrian "fascism" and that of the Nazis, and that it was not the charge of the western democracies to interfere in the struggle between the two fascist groups.

At any rate, the powers had no intention of confronting Hitler. From March of 1933 on, the fate of Austria lay entirely in the hands of the Italians. Had Italy not been prepared to intervene, Hitler, in 1934, would have intervened in Austria's battle against the insurgency of Austrian Nazis and German "tourists." When English policies concerning the Ethiopian question drove Italy into the arms of Hitler, the fate of Austria was sealed.

There are no words strong enough to describe the absurdity of English politics between the two wars. The English were unteachable. They believed they knew and understood everything better. They were mistrustful of everyone; but they believed everything the National Socialists said.

The behavior of the Czechs was even dumber. Even in 1938, Benes had seen in the restoration of the Hapsburg monarchy an evil greater than the *Anschluss*. The French took a position that was forthrightly sympathetic with Hitler. Nearly all educated Frenchmen were reading the *Gringoire*,[2] which openly defended Hitler. *Quos Deus vult perdere, dementat*.[3]

It was completely impossible to battle this stubbornness. When I went to Geneva I had hoped to be successful in contributing to the enlightenment of controlling personalities. But I soon came to realize that this was a futile undertaking. "We Englishmen," I was told by a member of the English Labour Party, "never want to wage war again." I asked: "And if Hitler should attack England?" The answer was bewildering: "Then we will just be ruled and exploited by German instead of English capitalists. It makes no difference to the people."

Since 1931, the League of Nations in Vienna was represented by a Dutchman named Rost van Tonningen. In Vienna,

---

[2]A right-wing French publication.

[3]"Those whom the Gods would destroy, they first make mad."

Rost openly advanced pro-Nazi propaganda. (When he later withdrew from the League of Nations and returned home, he was immediately appointed deputy führer of the National Socialist Party in the Netherlands.) My Viennese friends could not believe that it was impossible for me to achieve Rost's dismissal.

Only one nation had attempted serious opposition to Hitler on the European continent—the Austrian nation. It was only after five years of successful resistance that little Austria surrendered, abandoned by all. The whole world breathed a sigh of relief. Now Hitler would finally be satisfied; now he would deal peacefully with other nations. Twenty-seven months later, Hitler was the master of the European continent.

Index